PRISONER IN BAGHDAD

PRISONER IN BAGHDAD

Daphne Parish

with Pat Lancaster
and contributions from Michelle de Vries

CHAPMANS

For Martina and Michelle

Chapmans Publishers Ltd
141-143 Drury Lane
London WC2B 5TB

British Library Cataloguing in Publication Data

Parish, Daphne
Prisoner in Baghdad
I. Title   II. Lancaster, Pat
956.704092

ISBN 1 85592 633 4 (Hardback)
1 85592 613 X (C-format)

First Published by Chapmans 1992

Typeset by York House Typographic Ltd, London

Printed and bound in Great Britain by Clays Ltd, St Ives plc

Contents

A Breath of Fresh Air   1
A Day in the Country   17
Walls Have Ears   26
Solitary   44
Putting on the Pressure   57
A Very Special Message   73
Jingle Bells   94
Justice Will Be Done   101
A Toast to Freedom   118
Tell Dee I'm Sorry   124
Sisters in Prison   132
A Friend of my Own   153
Thoughts of Escape   167
On my Way   186
Living for Today   192
Acknowledgements   201

A Breath of Fresh Air

When I first met Farzad Bazoft in 1989, I was working as a nursing officer at the Ibn Al Bitar hospital in Baghdad – a challenging job that involved a much wider variety of tasks than its equivalent at home. As well as carrying out routine nursing duties, I was expected to act as all-round administrator during unsocial hours and to pour oil on troubled waters whenever a tricky situation, often to do with racial misunderstandings, arose. Demanding as it was, I enjoyed my work and counted myself fortunate to be living and working in the Middle East, an area that I had loved ever since my first assignment there in 1986.

There was only one nursing officer on duty at any given time at the Ibn Al Bitar during unsocial hours, and it was the sole responsibility of whoever was on to make sure the hospital ran smoothly. That could entail pacifying an irate patient, tracking down supplies of an unusual blood group for an urgent operation in theatre, or finding a plumber to repair an overflowing drain.

On a particularly busy Friday in late February I had coped with all those problems and more by 1.30 p.m. and had finally made it to the dining-room. I hadn't eaten at all that day – not even breakfast – and I was starving. Nurses are always advising people on the importance of regular mealtimes, but in my experience they are among the worst in the world at following their own advice. Have you ever noticed how many of them seem to survive on a diet of crisps and choco-late?

I was sitting at a table holding a telephone in one hand and forking food into my mouth with the other – I was trying to find a locum anaesthetist and had finally tracked him down to his hotel pool – when the bleep in the pocket of my uniform went off. I hurriedly swallowed a last mouthful of rice and made my way along the corridor, where I was informed that a journalist had arrived in reception and was asking to speak to someone about the hospital administration.

Though frustrated at having my lunch interrupted I knew how great a store both Parc, the Dublin-based company that managed the hospital, and the Iraqi authorities set by these public relations exercises, and I regarded them as part of my job. Parc was rightly proud of the up-to-date technology the hospital could provide and the Iraqis were anxious for the world to recognise that despite almost ten years of debilitating warfare with neighbouring Iran, the country was picking itself up, dusting itself off and providing a health service as good as any to be found in the West.

The Ibn Al Bitar had been a huge surprise when I'd first arrived in Baghdad. The hospital where I'd worked in Saudi Arabia had marble floors, fountained courtyards and beautiful paintings on the wall. The Ibn Al Bitar, in contrast, was grey and unimposing: a long, low single-storey L-shaped building. However, it enjoyed the highest reputation for efficiency among the local and expatriate communities alike. Many medics, like the anaesthetist I had just traced, made a point of putting in an intensive stint in the Ibn Al Bitar every year, in the hope of picking up new techniques from the multinational work-force.

So, I had conducted interviews of this kind before and I only wished, as I listened to my still-rumbling stomach, that I could have been given a little notice.

'Farzad Bazoft.' The journalist introduced himself with a wide smile and a firm handshake. 'I work for the *Observer* newspaper and I was wondering if you could tell me something about the hospital and how it operates, for an article we will be running on the reconstruction effort in Iraq. These two gentlemen,' he said, nodding his head left and right to indicate his official 'minders', 'are from the Ministry of Information.'

Bazoft looked about thirty years old. He was very tall, with dark hair, brown eyes and a relaxed manner. I took the three of them along to the staff dining-room for a cup of tea.

'Now, how can I help you? What do you want to know exactly?' I asked.

'Let's start with the sort of work you do here,' Bazoft said smoothly. 'The number of nurses you employ, the problems of nursing patients from a different culture who . . .'

'I'm sorry. I haven't the authority to talk about patients,' I replied, 'but I can give you a rundown on our specialities.'

I was well into my stride, waxing lyrical about the wonders of cardiac surgery and the operational success rate of the Ibn Al Bitar, when I became aware that Bazoft hadn't made a single note on his pad. Instead, he was looking at me with a sort of half-smile, his dark eyes flirting outrageously. He wasn't listening to a word I was saying! And why was he looking at me like that? He must be twenty years younger than me.

'And we have a renal ward which specialises in kidney transplants with a dialysis unit attached,' I finished lamely.

'That's wonderful,' said Bazoft, picking up his notepad and clipping his pen back into his jacket pocket. 'Er, can I telephone you later?' He smiled disarmingly.

'Yes, of course,' I said, caught off guard. 'But there isn't anything else I can tell you about the hospital that you couldn't read in our brochure. Perhaps you should get in touch with the hospital administrator – he could be of more help to you.' I gave him the telephone number and watched him make a note of it.

I escorted the three men back to the reception area and shook hands with them. As I closed the front door of the hospital Mohammed, a slightly-built member of the hospital's administration staff, stepped forward, barring my way.

3

'Miss Dee, I have relatives with me for more than half an hour. They have come to collect their father who died yesterday. They have a taxi waiting and are anxious to sign the relevant papers and take their father home.'

'But Mohammed,' I exclaimed, 'why didn't you bleep me? I would have come straightaway.'

'You were busy, Miss Dee, with very important people. Officers of the Ministry do not like to be interrupted. I would have been afraid.'

Afraid of what? I wondered, as I collected the death certificate, hospital record book and rubber stamp, before going to meet the dead man's male relatives. I knew that their womenfolk would be sitting by the roadside outside the mortuary gates in the stifling heat, awaiting the emergence of the coffin.

By the evening tea-break I was ready for a rest. In the dining-room I spotted Kitty and Susan, two members of staff with whom I was planning a trip to Basra and the marshes the weekend after next. Over tea, bread and jam we discussed our plans. We were all looking forward to the chance to unwind. The complete change of life-style offered by these weekends away was as beneficial as any rest. If only for a few hours, we were completely separated from the hospital environment. Living as we did, in apartment blocks populated only by other hospital staff, we were, in effect, almost permanently on call. But in the marshes and the desert we were as off duty as it was possible to be.

As Kitty, Susan and I chatted about the likelihood of bumping into friends in Basra, my bleep went off. I went to the switchboard where the operator told me there was an outside caller on the line.

'Hello, Dee, this is Farzad, Farzad Bazoft. Thank you for seeing me today. You were most helpful.'

'That's OK, no trouble at all,' I replied.

'Look, I was wondering if you would have dinner with me, tomorrow perhaps . . . '

I was amused. So I hadn't misread the signs – he had been making eyes at me. 'Would this be business, or pleasure?' I asked, with what I hoped was a friendly lilt to my voice. Why not meet this young man for dinner? He seemed nice enough, and I had nothing special on that evening. By now, I knew most of the expatriates in Baghdad. It would be a pleasant change to catch up on home news from a fresh perspective.

'What? . . . Oh, pleasure, of course,' Farzad replied. 'What about here at my hotel, the Mansour Melia? Is seven o'clock all right?'

'Seven o'clock would be fine.'

'Right, good, seven o'clock in the lobby. I look forward to it.'

As I replaced the receiver, my bleep sang out again.

'Miss Dee, please go to Ward C,' instructed the disembodied voice.

When I reached Ward C, I found it to be in total confusion. The relatives of several patients were standing about shouting and gesticulating at a young Irish nurse who had only recently arrived in the hospital. The upset had been caused by the nurse using as a doorstop a newspaper which carried a picture of Saddam Hussein on the front page. The relatives had seen her jamming it beneath a door and were mortified to see their President's picture subjected to this sort of treatment. Through an interpreter, I apologised for the distress they had been caused. Speaking in a soft and soothing voice, I explained that the young nurse was new to Baghdad and had not previously worked abroad; she hadn't known that treating Saddam Hussein's picture in that way was an unacceptable thing to do. In an attempt to placate them I invited the visitors to tea.

The entire fracas was watched by Abdullah. At around five foot seven in height and wearing his green army uniform, Abdullah was distinguishable from the other Iraqi soldiers who roamed the hospital twenty-four hours a day by the strange tufts of hair sprouting from his cheekbones and by his brown shoes. Rumour had it that soldiers who wore brown shoes, rather than black ones, were members of the élite Presidential Guard. There was also a belief that Abdullah had been assigned to the hospital for the sole purpose of relaying every detail of what took place there to the Presidential

Palace. This seemed to be borne out by his ability to smell out the action wherever it happened. Now, standing apart, his right hand on the gun at his hip, his narrowed eyes observed every aspect of the procedure in hand.

The family accepted my offer of tea and the nurse returned to her duties. I knew I would have to get the visitors' tea party over with in half an hour or I would be late handing over my report to the night shift at 8 p.m.

I eventually left the hospital at 9 p.m., having put in almost fourteen hours' work. I was tired, but not yet ready for sleep. I went home, had a quick bite to eat, showered, got into the hospital car that I had the use of, and drove across the Fourteenth of July Bridge to the British Club in Jazzaria. I always enjoyed driving through Baghdad at night. The heat of the day had eased, but it was still pleasantly warm and all the lights shone out over the River Tigris. How very lucky I was to be able to do the job I enjoyed and to be well rewarded for it, at a modern, well-equipped hospital in this exotic foreign city.

There was, as always, a lively crowd in the club tonight. Brits stood shoulder to shoulder with French, Yugoslav and American guests, lifting their glasses as they discussed the England-Wales rugby match, the Tour de France, the Australian Open. I greeted old friends, played snooker (I lost to an Austrian builder), and won at darts against two young Turkish men.

At home in bed I glanced at my watch and saw that it was midnight. Another Friday over. It had been no worse than any other Friday and a great deal better than some. And I had a date with a difference tomorrow night. I smiled to myself and reached over to switch off the light.

'Shall I wear something frilly and feminine, or should I go for the little black dress?' I asked my friend Catherine, who was sitting on my bed. I held each dress up against myself and looked in the mirror.

Catherine put her small, bird-like head on one side. 'It's Saturday night – I think you should dress up rather than play safe. The chiffon looks right to me.'

The chiffon was the colour of old rose, with a short tiered skirt, fitted bodice and shoe-string straps. Fortunately, it came with a matching jacket – even in the evening, exposed shoulders are unacceptable in the Arab world.

Catherine reached into my make-up box and selected rose-coloured lipstick and blusher, grey eye-shadow and charcoal mascara. 'You may as well stand out in the crowd,' she laughed. 'Most of the hospital staff will be at the Mansour Melia tonight.'

I dressed and made up carefully, sprayed a little Givenchy perfume on my skin and left the apartment block to walk the short distance past the Iraqi military training-ground and across the road to the Melia Hotel.

Farzad Bazoft was waiting in the lobby. He smiled as we shook hands.

'You look lovely, Dee – a vast improvement on the uniform,' he said, a reference to the bottle-green suit, white blouse and flat black shoes I had been wearing when we'd met at the hospital. We moved into the hotel bar, known as the 'clinic' because it was frequented by so many hospital staff.

'Would you like a drink?' he asked.

'Please, Dubonnet on ice, no lemon.'

'And a Scotch and water for me,' Farzad said. The waiter smiled as he took the order.

'You're not Iraqi, are you?' Farzad enquired.

'No sir, I am from Cairo. All the Iraqi men are in the army and we Egyptians provide cheap labour. Where are you from, sir?'

'England – I'm here on business.'

When the waiter returned with our drinks he spoke softly as he leaned to place the glasses on the low table in front of us. Inclining his head towards Farzad, he said, 'If you have dollars I can give you a good exchange rate, sir.'

I shook my head warningly at Farzad. Dealing on the black market was a punishable offence.

'Thanks, Cairo,' he responded cheerfully, 'but I didn't bring any dollars with me. Maybe next time.'

The waiter melted away. I started to protest, but Farzad cut me short. 'I know what you're going to say. You're going to warn me about the penalties for selling foreign currency, but you know, Dee, I don't think the authorities really care about people exchanging money on the black market. In the six years that I have travelled in and out of Iraq, I haven't heard of a single person being prosecuted. Have you?'

I moved to a safer subject. 'You must have met some interesting people if you've been coming here for six years.'

'Well, no, not really,' Farzad replied. 'All my previous visits were during the Iran-Iraq War and I wasn't allowed to move around outside the hotel unless escorted by an Iraqi official which, as you can imagine, is a bit restricting.' He smiled broadly. 'Being able to meet people and socialise on this visit made all the difference. By the way, do you know any of the British Embassy staff here? Have you met the First Secretary, Robin Kealy?'

'Yes, I think so, briefly, at a garden party a few months ago. He's the very tall chap, isn't he, slim with light-brown, wavy hair?'

'That's him,' Farzad said. 'Well, he runs an amateur dramatics group at his home. They are doing a play tomorrow and he's invited me to go along. Would you like to come with me?'

'Yes,' I replied. 'It sounds fun.'

We moved into the dining-room and selected a table overlooking the manicured lawns and floodlit swimming-pool in the hotel grounds. A Filipina waitress brought a selection of hors d'oeuvres and we tucked in. Throughout the meal Farzad entertained me with outrageous stories of the newspaper world. He was intelligent, quick-witted and amusing; I felt completely at ease with him.

'So, Dee, tell me about yourself. Are you married?'

'No, not any more, though I have been. What about you?'

'No – one day, I hope, but not yet. Do you have children?'

'I have two daughters – well, one is actually my stepdaughter.'

'And what brings you to Iraq?' Farzad went on.

'The same thing that brings everyone initially, I suppose – money. After my second marriage broke up I bought a flat in

North London and then found that it was costing me only slightly less to run than I was earning. I had no furniture to speak of – no curtains, no bed and no real hopes of getting them. Martina, my stepdaughter, was in student accommodation and although my daughter, Michelle, was living in the flat with me, I rarely saw her: I was working shifts and she has a fairly hectic social life. She'll be twenty-one soon. So when I saw an advertisement in the *Nursing Times* for nurses in Saudi Arabia, I applied and got the job.'

'Saudi Arabia?'

'Yes, that's where I went first. I spent two years there before coming to Iraq last year.'

'How did you find life in Saudi then?'

'I enjoyed it, for the most part. It was restrictive outside the compounds where the expatriates live, with women having to remain covered from head to toe and not being allowed to drive, but inside those high compound fences we had a lot of fun. And I really shouldn't complain, because working there allowed me to buy carpets and a three-piece suite, even though I'm not in London to enjoy them.'

'You obviously relish the expatriate life-style, Dee – have you lived anywhere else apart from Iraq and Saudi Arabia?'

'Not for years. When I was first married I lived in the Bahamas and we travelled around quite a bit in those days, but that was for pleasure, not work.'

'A bit of a jet-setter then, are we, Dee?' Farzad said, laughing.

'Maybe once, but not any more. I'm just a hard-working nurse with a mortgage to find.'

'I know the feeling, not of being a nurse, but of having a mortgage round your neck. I've just bought a place in North London myself.'

We talked about home and Farzad explained how he would like to decorate his flat, starkly in black and white, and furnish it with clean, sharp lines and state-of-the-art stereo equipment.

At around midnight Farzad escorted me back to my apartment block and we shook hands at the lift door.

'Until tomorrow then, Dee!' he said. 'Seven o'clock in the hotel lobby.'

He smiled, gave a little wave and was gone.

Robin Kealy lived in a spacious house near the exclusive racecourse area of Baghdad. The amateur theatre group was nearing the end of the three-act play by the time Farzad and I were ushered into the sitting-room: we had decided to have a drink before leaving the hotel, and had ended up talking about all sorts of things, from our respective jobs to stereo systems. As we took our seats, we whispered greetings to Robin and his wife, Annabelle, who were sitting among a group of about thirty-five expatriates, mostly British, watching six actors on stage. I groaned inwardly as one of the actors went through the motions of a cardiac arrest – this was too much like a busman's holiday. The play drew to a close amid laughter and clapping and we joined the other guests in queueing at a long table for shepherd's pie and salad.

Robin, a charming and sophisticated man, introduced us to the cast and other members of the audience. Some of the expatriates there hadn't heard of the Ibn Al Bitar hospital and assumed they would fly home if they developed a serious medical problem. While this is all right in theory, it is not necessarily practical or advisable, and I spent much of the evening performing another public relations job for the hospital.

'You really should make emergency plans,' I found myself saying. 'If you were involved in a car crash, there simply wouldn't be time to fly you home.' As I spread sunshine around the gathering, speaking of accidents and heart attacks, Farzad chatted with the guests, always on the lookout for interesting titbits or stories.

We left at about 11.30 p.m., picked up a cruising taxi and headed back to the apartment block.

'Dee, I'm sorry to say this is my last evening in Iraq,' Farzad said. 'I have to catch the morning flight. I was wondering – do you think we could meet up some time when you're in London? When is your next leave?'

'At the end of next month – British Airways are offering low-cost flights at the moment. I'll be home for a week on 25 March.'

Farzad scribbled down two telephone numbers on a sheet of paper torn from his diary.

'This is my telephone number at home, and the *Observer* number is underneath. You'll be able to get me at one or the other. Be sure to ring, won't you?' he said with a grin.

I smiled back at him. Of course I would keep in touch. His arrival in Baghdad had been like a breath of fresh air. At the time, most of the people I knew there were involved in very specific professions – medicine, engineering, construction – mainly expatriate labour brought in to fulfil Iraq's post-war needs. Farzad made journalism sound such a dynamic, racy kind of job that I felt I would never tire of hearing his stories – it was a whole new experience for me.

There were very few unattached expatriate women in Baghdad whereas there were thousands of men from all over western Europe, North America and the Eastern bloc nations. Whatever a woman's age or physical appearance, she would always be in demand. Some women would have as many as three dates on a single Saturday night. It wasn't one vast orgy – on the contrary, most of the relationships were very circumspect: the men were just pleased to have a woman's company for a couple of hours. Entering a club or bar with a female on their arm afforded them considerable kudos with their friends and colleagues, as it would in any city where men outnumbered women by around three hundred to one. But even with these odds, Farzad was special, although it was never on the cards that our relationship would be a serious one. It was more like a holiday romance, started in Baghdad and later nurtured in London.

When I returned to England in March I telephoned him at the

Observer. He sounded delighted to hear from me and invited me to join him at his office the following day.

I had expected to see lots of sawdust and huge black presses thumping away churning out pages of newspaper as fast as the eye could see, so it was something of a surprise to find Farzad in a light, airy office which had carpets on the floor and potted plants dotted around.

'Sorry to disappoint you, Dee, but everything is done by computer nowadays,' he explained. 'The point is, we no longer need to be in the same building as the printers. There are a lot of advantages to the new technology – it makes life much easier for the journalists – but some of the older guys, those who worked in Fleet Street, say they miss the camaraderie.'

I thoroughly enjoyed my guided tour around the offices of a national newspaper. Farzad was playing the ace reporter, showing me 'proofs' of pages that would appear in the next issue. 'Don't tell anyone you've seen these,' he said conspiratorially, though we both knew I had no intention of running off to some rival publication to spill the beans. But it added to the aura of glamour and intrigue he was trying to build up, not particularly around himself, but around the job he enjoyed so much.

I was not looking for a lover in Farzad, but we developed a closeness in our relationship that made the final step almost an inevitable one. The next day we met up in the afternoon and spent hours walking together on Hampstead Heath. I can't remember now all the topics we discussed, but conversation was never a problem for us. He told me in wonderful, gossipy detail about all the people I had met at his office the previous day, and expressed his hopes of getting a permanent staff job. Taken on by the *Observer* during the Iran-Iraq War as a freelance with a desk, he was banking on the position being formalised soon. He was, he reckoned, just as good at his job as most of his colleagues, and better than some.

We had supper in a restaurant on Devonshire Hill.

'It's great to see you again, Dee,' said Farzad, taking my

hand across the table. 'I've thought about you a lot. When are you coming back to England for good?'

'Never,' I laughed. 'It's much too cold. I need sunshine and year-round swimming. Ideally, I would like to move from Iraq to Bahrain or Abu Dhabi, then I could sail, too. I love the sea almost as much as the desert. In either of those countries I would have both.'

'Why are you so fascinated by desert countries?' Farzad asked.

'I don't really know the answer to that, but you're right, I do find them fascinating. Have you ever driven through the desert?'

Farzad shook his head.

'Well, at first sight it looks as if there is nothing there, nothing but sand in every direction. You need a four-wheel drive vehicle, a compass and a lot of food and water to venture into it, because it's so easy to get lost. You should never underestimate the desert, it's a constantly changing thing. In the daylight it's bakingly hot, but the temperature falls dramatically at night. You can be out driving and it seems as if there is nothing at all but sand between you and the horizon, when suddenly, out of nowhere it seems, you'll see a herd of camels, perhaps a hundred or more. They won't move, so you have to circumnavigate them – and this is when you might come across a Bedouin tent, miles away from any-where. Barefoot children will spill out of the doorway, shout-ing "Pepsi, Pepsi!" The women will peep around the door and an old man might hobble forward to shake your hand, give a broad, toothless grin and say, "*Marhaba* (Welcome)!"

'There might be a dozen goats nearby of varying colours, with piebald and skewbald patterning such as one doesn't see in Europe. As you look at all the sand around, you wonder what on earth they find to eat. These days, Bedouins drive Land Rovers and shop at supermarkets like everyone else, but I often wonder how they used to manage years ago, before the discovery of oil, when the Gulf states were poor and barren countries – how did they sustain themselves?'

I suddenly realised that I was going on a bit, as I often do when I start talking about the desert.

Farzad smiled. 'Well, for the moment I'll have to take your word for it. Maybe next time I'm in Iraq you can show me some of these amazing sights. You see, quite stupidly, I thought the desert was just sand, sand and more sand.'

'Then you're in for a treat,' I assured him.

We left the restaurant and took a taxi back to his flat. He had told me a great deal about his plans for it, but I hadn't realised how few of them had materialised. There was very little furniture, but until he could afford the expensive items he had set his heart on, he was, he explained, happy to make do. I loved his confidence. An hour earlier he had been explaining how important it was to him to get a staff position on the *Observer*. There was, it seemed, no doubt in his mind that he would achieve this; it was really only a question of when. This was just the next rung of a ladder that would allow him to fit out his home in the way he wanted and take him right to the top of his chosen career.

Farzad was asleep by the time I tiptoed out of his flat in the early hours of the morning. Two days later I returned to Iraq, without having managed to see him again.

After my seven-day holiday in England I returned to Iraq, but flew back to London at the beginning of June for Michelle's twenty-first birthday.

'Everything is arranged,' said my daughter, airily waving a hand. 'All you have to do, Mummy, is turn up and enjoy yourself – but don't dance with all the young boys!'

The party, arranged by her boyfriend Peter, was to be held at an exclusive club in Mayfair. Michelle looked beautiful in a long, cream silk dress, which complemented her golden skin and long dark hair. She stood with Peter receiving her guests. They came from all walks of life – stockbrokers, actors, lawyers, well-known faces from the music world (people she'd met as a result of her work), as well as long-lost cousins and all the old folk. I was one of the latter, but I didn't let it restrain me – I whirled around the dance floor at every opportunity. In between dances I shared a table with my stepdaughter Martina and Peter's mother, Billie.

Midnight struck and Peter stood up to propose a toast to Michelle. As we sang 'Happy Birthday' my mind flashed back twenty-one years to the day Michelle was born, in the Antoni Clinic on Grand Bahama island. Cory, my first husband, and I had been so convinced she would be a boy that we didn't even have a name for a daughter. I had a difficult labour and Michelle was eventually delivered by Caesarian section. I wasn't well after the birth and for several days I was unable to see her. I remembered Cory sitting on my bed as we discussed what we should call her.

'What about Michelle?' I suggested.

'Michelle . . . yes, I like that,' he said. 'We'll call her Michelle.'

'Let's not rush it – does she look like a Michelle?'

He frowned. 'I don't know, how do Michelles look?'

'Oh, Cory, just go down to the nursery and look at her. You'll see if she looks like a Michelle or not.'

Reluctantly, I felt, he left to go to the nursery. Within five minutes he was back, grinning all over his face.

'Yes,' he said, nodding his head emphatically. 'She definitely looks like a Michelle.' In fact, when I eventually saw her three days later, I thought she looked more like Winston Churchill.

I was so wrapped up in my thoughts that I almost failed to hear what Michelle was saying. Suddenly a gasp went around the room. I looked up to see that she was on her feet and smiling broadly: she had just announced that she and Peter were to be married. Friends were rushing forward to congratulate the happy couple. Billie and I remained seated and sized each other up: after all, we would soon be related.

The rest of my holiday flew by as we discussed wedding invitations, the colour of the dress I would wear and where the ceremony would take place. I tried telephoning Farzad at home but there was no reply, and I didn't get around to calling again. Shortly before I left, Michelle and I had a minor disagreement that turned into a major row. Planning a wedding is never easy, and we were both overwrought. As I left England I was comforted by the thought that Peter would take care of her and iron out any emotional creases I might have created.

It was three months later, on Friday 8 September, that I next heard from Farzad. The phone rang early in the morning in my apartment in Baghdad. Still half-asleep I opened my eyes and reached for the receiver.

'Dee, hi, it's Farzad . . . Yes, it is a bit of a surprise. The government invited me back to cover the Kurdish elections. Can we meet? Tonight? That's great, I'll pick you up at eight o'clock.'

A Day in the Country

It was wonderful to see him again. He looked fit and well, and was obviously excited about something. We sat on my sofa sipping ice-cold daiquiris.

'Come on, Farzad, spit it out. I know you're bursting to tell me something! What is it? What's happened?'

He grinned broadly, but for a moment he didn't speak. Then, choosing his words carefully, he asked, 'Have you heard anything about a big explosion in Iraq?'

'No,' I replied. 'What sort of explosion, whereabouts and what caused it?'

'It was somewhere between Baghdad and Basra – the *Independent* newspaper carried the story.'

We were interrupted by a knock at the door. It was my friend Catherine, who had stopped by for an impromptu visit. I wondered if she might know something.

'Catherine, Farzad has just asked me if I have heard about an explosion. I haven't heard anything – have you?'

'No, nothing.' She looked over at Farzad. 'What was it – a bomb?'

'I don't know exactly, but there is a rumour that seven hundred people were killed. It may have been a munitions factory or something, but if you should hear anything about it, let me know. I'd like to get to the bottom of it while I'm here on the spot.'

'I'll be seeing a friend of mine who's with the peacekeeping force this evening. I'll ask him if he's heard anything,' Catherine promised.

Shortly after Catherine left, I drove Farzad over the Arbah Bridge to the Meridian Hotel, where a number of foreign journalists, in Iraq like Farzad to cover the Kurdish elections, were staying. We had dinner and moved on to the bar, where the journalists had gathered to discuss the problems of getting worthwhile stories out of a country obsessed with secrecy. Farzad made the introductions. All the journalists were interested in the explosion story, but none of them seemed to know what had happened.

Two days later Farzad was back at my apartment. I could see he was agitated and he strode up and down, running his fingers through his hair. The Ministry of Information had promised to provide him with transport to visit the so-called explosion site, but the car had not turned up at the agreed time. He had spent the day in his hotel room, waiting, phoning the Ministry and being told a car was on its way. It never arrived.

'They promised, the assholes, they promised to send a car and now every other journalist in Iraq has been there except me. Yesterday the boys from ITN climbed over the fence that runs around the site. It got them into a spot of bother, in fact they were arrested for the day, but at least they got a story. What are they going to say at the *Observer*? They will all be sitting in the office right now saying, "Where's our lad, then? What's Farzad been up to since he arrived there?"'

'Farzad,' I ventured at last, 'it looks to me as if the Ministry has no intention of sending a car. Why don't you take a taxi and go tomorrow morning – that's not too late, surely?'

'Because the site is out of Baghdad, at a place called Hilla. A taxi would never find it. The driver would cruise around for God knows how long, tell me he couldn't find it, shrug his shoulders and charge me twenty dinar for having wasted my day. You know what these people are like, Dee. Most of the taxi-drivers in Baghdad are just simple folk from the villages; they can't even read or write.'

I could see he was at the end of his tether and I felt sorry for him. He obviously thought he was the only journalist in Iraq who had not been to Hilla, and it didn't fit with the hot-shot reporter image he had of himself.

Suddenly it entered my head that I might be able to help out. Tomorrow was my day off and aside from a tennis match, tentatively arranged with Catherine, and maybe an amble through the bazaar, I had nothing planned.

'Look, Farzad, would you like me to drive you there? I have a couple of days off starting tomorrow.'

He beamed at me. 'Do you know where it is?'

'Well, no, not exactly, but I have a rough idea and we could ask, couldn't we? Anyway, I won't drive you round in a circle and charge you twenty dinar.'

He laughed and gave me a quick hug. 'Dee, you're an angel. That would be great.'

'There's just one thing, Farzad. I don't want any fence-climbing or anything that might get us into trouble. It's OK for your pals from ITN, they'll be leaving in a few days, but I have to work here. So, are we agreed?'

'Absolutely!' Farzad shook his head from side to side; all the agitation seemed to fall away from him as he anticipated tomorrow and what he might find at Hilla. Farzad, I thought to myself, in some ways you're just like a little boy.

The following morning I packed a cool-box with water, soft drinks, two cans of beer and some snacks. I had checked the tyres of the car, the oil, water and spare wheel and, since I'd be driving a hospital vehicle, I'd told the hospital office where I would be going. By 10 a.m. I was at Farzad's hotel to collect him.

We headed south on the Hilla road, which was clearly signposted. Farzad was in good spirits and had a stack of jokes to tell. He was the perfect companion for a ride in the country this lovely, sunny morning.

'Hey Dee, have you heard the one about the man who couldn't stop eating concrete?'

'No.'

'He was permanently stoned.'

'Have you heard the one about the wood-louse who lived in a brick? Have you heard . . . ?'

When we reached the outskirts of Hilla we stopped. Where now? A group of local people were walking towards us in the long, white Arab-style gowns known as djellabas, their heads covered in red-and-white-checked cloths (keffiyehs). Farzad poked his head out of the window and spoke to them in broken Arabic.

'*Hamza* kilometres,' replied one of the men, pointing along the road. We started up again, and I checked off five kilometres on the dashboard clock. We scanned the horizon. Suddenly Farzad jumped up in the passenger seat and nudged my arm.

'There, look, Dee, off to the right a bit further down the road, I can see some barbed wire. Turn off here.'

I drove off the main highway and threaded through minor tracks until we reached the barbed-wire fence. There was very little to see, just a few trees and then scrubland stretching to the horizon.

'Let's follow the fence around,' Farzad suggested.

We drove on until we came to a gate guarded by a middle-aged man with a huge pot belly, who sauntered up to the car and said 'Good morning' in English. Farzad spoke to him through the car window. I saw the guard wave over his shoulder towards the gate behind him and heard him say, 'One kilometre.' Farzad thanked him and we drove away.

I'd kept the engine running and hadn't managed to catch much of the conversation.

'What did he say?' I asked Farzad as we drove on.

'He said that this is the site of the explosion. They don't know what caused it, but many people died. We're not allowed to go through the gate, so we might as well go back to Baghdad.'

He looked very downcast as we drove away. I knew he felt that if he had managed to get to the site yesterday or the day before, at the same time as all the other journalists, he would have been able to cobble some sort of a story together for his paper, but it all looked a bit hopeless now.

Suddenly he gripped my arm. 'Stop a minute, I've just seen something interesting!' I pulled over to the side of the road. 'Can you back up a bit?'

I reversed the car slowly up the empty road until I drew level with the object of Farzad's attention. He was staring at what looked like a pile of coal-dust dumped on the grass verge at the side of the road. He was muttering excitedly to himself. 'Interesting, very, very interesting!' He sounded like some loony professor.

He turned to look at me. 'Let's go somewhere, I want to think. This could have come from the explosion.'

Privately, I thought Farzad was allowing himself to be carried away by a fantasy, but we drove to a tea-house further along the route, where we were served tea Arab-style, in tiny glasses half-filled with sugar. Farzad got into conversation with a local schoolteacher and as fresh tea was brought, I wandered over to an open window. A man was sitting outside on a bench. He looked up at me and smiled.

'Hello! Are you English? I speak a little English.' He then proceeded to tell me how he had lost his left leg in the war. 'It make much *alum* (pain), I not *imshee* (walk) good.'

I smiled at him. I had seen many men like him in Iraq, who had lost limbs fighting against Iran. It seemed such a waste – what had it been for? After almost ten years and thousands of deaths on both sides there had still been no resolution. I didn't, of course, say any of this to my one-legged friend, but even so, in the coming weeks my innocent conversation with him was to be twisted out of all recognition.

Farzad put his hand on my shoulder. 'Time to go, Dee. I'm due at a press conference at two o'clock.'

He was quiet and thoughtful on the journey home. I sang songs from the musical *Oliver* but he didn't join in. He was, I supposed, deeply disappointed.

I was surprised to hear from Farzad again that evening: he telephoned as I was getting ready to go out with a group of friends. I was even more surprised to hear him say he wanted to return to Hilla the following day. He seemed to think there might be something around the back of the explosion site, someting the other journalists had overlooked. I didn't have anything else on so I agreed to take him back.

When he arrived at 10.15 the next morning, I was packing the cool-box. He wandered around looking at the pictures and photographs on the walls of my apartment.

'Tell me more about your children,' he said.

'Well, as I told you, I have one daughter, Michelle, and one stepdaughter, Martina. Michelle was born in the Bahamas when I was married to my first husband, Cory de Vries, and Martina, the daughter of my second husband, John Parish, was eight years old when I first met her. They are very different.'

'In what way?' Farzad asked.

'Oh, in almost every way imaginable. Michelle is dark-haired and blue-eyed and very striking. She has a quick mind and a phenomenal memory for facts and figures. She works as a manager and agent for a rock group and lives with her boyfriend, Peter, in London. Martina is blonde and blue-eyed, a kind, attractive girl with a sweet nature and a wonderful sense of humour. She's a staff nurse at a London hospital but the two girls rarely meet up. It's not that they don't get on together, it's just that they have very little in common.'

'That's a bit sad,' said Farzad thoughtfully. 'What about your relationship with them?'

'It would be difficult not to get on with Martina, she has such an easy-going nature, but I get on well with Michelle too – we have arguments, of course, because we're both strong-willed people, but we are very close.'

'I hope I'll meet them one day,' Farzad said. 'Have you finished getting ready? Here, let me carry the cool-box. By the way, have you got a couple of empty containers I could use?'

'What sort of containers – lemonade bottles, cardboard boxes or what?'

'No, something smaller, if you have it.'

'I have a couple of small pots, part of a damaged batch of containers delivered to the hospital. They were no longer sterile, so I thought I would hang on to a couple to use for hand cream when I go on holiday.'

'Yes, they sound fine.'

I gave him the two pots with Ibn Al Bitar labels wrapped around them and he slipped them into the pocket of his jeans.

We followed the same route as we had the previous day and arrived at the explosion site. I continued to drive along the main road.

'Hey, where are you going?' Farzad shouted. 'You've over-shot the turn-off.'

'I thought you wanted to go round to the back of the site. I'm looking for the next road off.'

'No, no, turn around and go back. I want to be where we were yesterday.'

We reached the pile of ash by the side of the road. Further along, on the other side, was a mound of earth with a soldier standing on top, holding a gun – but this was not an unusual sight in Iraq. The hospital was surrounded by soldiers: they were posted at street corners and on top of mounds and roof-tops throughout the city.

Outside the explosion site cars passed up and down the road on which we were parked. Farzad got out of the car and stared down at the pile of ash he had noticed the day before. It was a hot day. I reached into the cool-box and rummaged around for a soda, flipped back the metal tag and drank deeply. Farzad returned to the car holding an old shoe and a lump of rock.

'You're not thinking of putting that filthy old thing into my car!' I exclaimed with distaste. Really, journalists were quite extraordinary people. A truck passed by, cutting in so sharply that it almost took away my front bumper.

'Idiot driver!' I yelled at the disappearing truck.

The soldier on the mound opposite looked over at us but showed no interest. Farzad climbed back into the car, opened the glove compartment, threw something in and said, 'Come on, Dee, let's get back. I've got another press conference at two o'clock.'

As I moved off, Farzad reached into his bag and produced a camera. There were no signs to indicate that we were in a sensitive area and that photography was banned – another common sight in Iraq. He took a snap of a road sign, which read 'Alexandria' in English with the Arabic equivalent beneath, and two other pictures of scrubland and the perimeter fence.

We headed north, back to Baghdad. Farzad was in high spirits and the drive home was much cheerier than it had been the previous day. He had a fresh collection of jokes and we laughed and sang together like children.

It seemed that in no time at all we were back at the Fourteenth of July Bridge. My mind went blank for a second and I pulled the car over to the side of the road so that I could determine which side of the bridge we were on. If I was going in the wrong direction it was better to know now, before I found myself in the midst of a busy lunchtime snarl-up of irate drivers. In a flash a policeman appeared at the car window.

'What you do? Why you stop?' he shouted in my face. 'Where you go? Who are you?'

I realised with a sickly feeling in the pit of my stomach that I had pulled up in front of the palace grounds, the home of President Saddam Hussein.

'I'm dreadfully sorry, officer,' I stammered. 'I had a brainstorm. I couldn't remember which side of the bridge I was on. But I know where I am now.'

'You not stop here. Where you go? What you do?'

'We were just on our way to the Meridian Hotel. My friend is due at a press conference in half an hour.'

The policeman glowered but waved us on. As we pulled away I looked out of my rear-view mirror and spotted him writing something down in a notebook.

'You are an idiot,' Farzad hissed. 'If he had searched the car, he would have found my camera.'

'So what?' I retorted, stung by his brusqueness. 'There's no law against carrying a camera. Iraq is supposed to be the cradle of civilisation, the country is heaving with ancient monuments. As long as we don't point our cameras at buildings carrying a sign saying photography forbidden there's no problem. I carry a camera all the time.'

Later, I was deeply to regret having made that last statement.

Two days later, on Thursday evening, I received a call from Farzad asking me to meet him in the bar of the Sheraton Hotel.

'How long have you got?' he asked when I arrived.

'About an hour, Farzad. I've just put in a gruelling fourteen-hour stint at the hospital and I'm on duty again at 7.30 tomorrow morning.'

'It was good of you to come, Dee. This isn't something I wanted to say over the telephone.'

I sat back in my chair and waited for him to speak.

'I will be leaving tomorrow,' he announced abruptly. 'The British Embassy have advised me to get out.'

'Why, what on earth has happened?'

'I offered them the ash samples I picked up at Hilla to take out in the diplomatic bag. They refused and advised me to get out of Iraq as soon as possible. I'm catching the first plane out tomorrow.'

'You weren't planning to leave until Tuesday, were you? Are you in trouble, Farzad?'

'No, nothing like that. The Embassy said it wasn't the sort of thing they put in their diplomatic bag, but it's not a problem, Dee. Just forget it – everything's fine. Anyway, how are you?'

'On top of the world. My December holiday was confirmed today. I'm going to be home for Christmas.'

He took my hands and we laughed together. 'That's tremendous, Dee! Let's get together. Ring me as soon as you get to Heathrow.'

'Of course.'

The rest of our conversation was taken up with discussing our respective plans for Christmas. Farzard walked me to the car park and waved as I drove away. He had told me the weather in London was fine, but I felt sure it would be nowhere near as good as the sunny days we had been enjoying in Iraq, and I resolved to sort myself out some warm clothes for my trip home in December.

Walls Have Ears

Attempting to resuscitate someone after a cardiac arrest is always an enormous drain on mental and physical energy, whatever the outcome. Today the patient had been a young woman with a rare disease; it had taken four of us a full hour to bring her round. I felt exhausted as I made my way back to the nursing office, but I still had some paperwork to do: I had to work out next week's duty rota for the thirty-five Iraqi interpreters employed at the hospital. This presented no easy task. For cultural reasons all the night interpreters had to be male, so organising the night shift was comparatively plain sailing; but since three of the women were on maternity leave, a further two were on long-term sick leave, and one flatly refused to work anywhere other than in the renal clinic, the day rota took some working out. What's more, some departments refused to accept certain characters on the rota, while others were so highly specialised that they needed interpreters who were experienced in their particular field. Just as I was beginning to make sense of it all my bleep sounded.

'Miss Dee, please go to Dr Raad's office, quickly!' the voice instructed.

Now what? I wondered, as I walked the full length of the hospital over to outpatients where Dr Raad, the Iraqi Chief Administrator, had his offices.

'Go straight in,' said the secretary. 'There are some people waiting to see you.'

People? What people? I hoped this wouldn't take long; I

already had more than enough to do without having to conduct any unexpected guests on a guided tour of the hospital. Dr Raad stood behind his desk: he seemed to be reading from a sheet of paper. Two men dressed in dark suits sat in chairs at opposite ends of the desk. Dr Raad looked up, his expression serious.

'Dee, you have to go and see the judge. These men have come to take you there by car,' he said quietly.

Judge? What was he talking about? Was this mysterious judge ill? In any event, I couldn't leave the hospital now.

'Sorry, that's impossible,' I replied firmly. 'I can't go any-where, I'm on call for cardiac arrest. What is this all about anyway?'

'I don't know,' he replied, but whatever was written in Arabic on the paper he held before him had clearly caused him concern. Even the hospital's Chief Administrator was not exempt from fear of Iraqi officialdom. It was a fear I had seen on many occasions during the course of my work, on the faces of both patients and staff. An invidious sort of 'walls have ears' fear that I now know I had never really understood, putting it down to some kind of national paranoia. 'But you must go with these men, now,' he added.

I began to feel vague stirrings of discomfort, although I tried not to let them show.

'Before I can go anywhere I will have to call the Director of Nursing. I can't just ignore the fact I'm on call for cardiac arrest and walk out of the hospital. Besides, I'm not prepared to get into a car with two men I've never set eyes on before,' I said, briskly.

Dr Raad spoke in Arabic to the men before returning his gaze to me. He pointed to the telephone on his desk. 'You may ring the Director of Nursing from here.'

As I listened to the ringing tone, waiting for the Director of Nursing to answer, I desperately searched my mind for an explanation. I was genuinely puzzled. What could an Iraqi judge possibly want with me? Then it came to me – the car accident, of course, that must be it!

The previous Saturday evening the car in which I had been

travelling as a passenger had been hit from behind by a mad driver in a bright green car, who then screeched off as if nothing had happened. No one had been injured, and since minor collisions were part and parcel of the generally poor standard of driving in Baghdad, I had thought nothing of it. Or, could it be about the Ambassador? An Iraqi Ambassador, who had served in the West, a patient in Ward C1, had recently slipped and fallen on a wet bathroom floor; had he made a complaint? Or maybe the Iraqi General in Ward E: he seemed pleasant enough, but one never knew who was going to complain about what and to whom. After a year at the Ibn Al Bitar hospital I was under no illusions: if anything went wrong anywhere in the hospital it was us, the nursing staff, who were expected to carry the can.

At last the Director of Nursing picked up her telephone. I quickly explained the situation and my reluctance to get into a car with two strange men. 'Quite right,' she answered reassuringly. 'Sit tight, Dee, I'm on my way over.'

Dr Raad looked not only worried but also a little scared. 'You must go now, Dee. These men cannot wait.'

I looked at him. He couldn't be serious. He didn't really expect me to drive away with these two strangers, after some of the stories I had heard from other expatriates in Iraq. Rumours of Western women being taken into the desert – raped, murdered, buried in the sand and never heard of again – were rife in Baghdad. There may not have been a shred of truth in the tales, but I had no desire to conduct any personal research.

I appealed to Dr Raad, whom I had always considered a reasonable and compassionate man. 'If I have to go, I can't go alone. Come with me, please! If you don't, who knows where I may end up?'

The two men stood up and moved towards me. 'We go now,' one of them said in English. 'Dr Raad can come with you.' I couldn't believe what was happening. If only I could speak to the Director of Nursing. She was a sensible woman in a responsible position; perhaps they would take some notice of her. I asked to visit the washroom – a delaying tactic as much as anything else. As I left Dr Raad's office, one of the men followed me down the corridor and positioned himself right outside the loo door. At that moment I felt fear for the first time. Up until then it had seemed as if these were just a couple of guys messing up my day with their nonsense. Now, suddenly, it felt very serious indeed. Otherwise what was this man following me around for, standing right outside the loo door as if I was about to run away or something?

As the four of us walked out of the hospital, we passed the Director of Nursing on her way to see me. She put up a hand in protest but I was swept right past her, and into the back seat of a waiting car. She stared after us as the car sped out of the hospital grounds.

The driver clearly did not want me to know where I was going. He turned in and out of narrow back streets, taking roundabout routes and frequently doubling back on himself. It was all a waste of time, because as a driver I knew Baghdad very well by this time. Even though there were few street names visible (these had been removed at the outset of Iraq's war with Iran, to foil any would-be invasion attempt), I was able to recognise many of the shops and buildings. I knew I was in the area of Karrada, a long shopping street where Arab paintings and *objets d'art* were frequently sought by Western expatriates.

We entered a gate and drew up beside a sort of prefabricated hut. A tall, good-looking soldier escorted us inside. From the Arabic conversation that ensued I understood that his name was Ahmed. One of the young men was speaking to Dr Raad in what sounded like a fairly official tone, but I was unprepared for what followed.

'I have to go now, Dee,' Dr Raad told me quietly. 'They say I must leave.'

I panicked. I didn't want to be left alone in this hut with these young boys in uniform. 'No! No, don't leave me, please don't leave me!' I implored.

'I have to, Dee. I'm sorry, but they say I'm not allowed to stay. We will contact the British Embassy, who will inform your family.' Then he was gone. I heard the sound of the car engine – I was on my own.

'Does anyone speak English?' I looked around hopefully, but was met with only blank stares. Other soldiers came into the hut or stood at the door looking at me with curiosity. Although compared with Saudi Arabia Iraq had seemed to me to be a very liberal, almost Westernised country most of the time, it is still part of the Arab world, with that world's culture and traditions. These boys would not be accustomed to seeing lone women outside of their immediate family; that was clear from the way they stared at me, taking in every detail, especially the blonde hair and blue eyes.

Female virtue is a highly-prized commodity in the Arab world. To ensure the good behaviour of men, women are required to make special efforts, which often include keeping themselves covered from head to foot when outside the home. Women are rarely seen walking in the street unaccompanied either by another woman or a male family member. Of course, different Arab countries have a different approach to these traditions. In Saudi Arabia and Iran it is compulsory to cover up, whereas in other countries, such as Egypt and Jordan, it is left to the discretion of the individual. But throughout the Islamic world these customs are particularly prevalent among the rural population and ordinary working-class people from families such as the ones these boys probably came from.

The soldiers spoke among themselves, sometimes loudly, sometimes quietly, obviously about me. There were eight or perhaps ten of them. The fact that none admitted to speaking English compounded my fear, although why should rape or murder be any more devastating in a foreign language?

I realised that Dr Raad was the only person who knew where I was. Because he was Iraqi and so obviously scared, to what extent, I wondered, could I depend on him to do as he had promised and contact the British Embassy? I felt frightened, alone and physically vulnerable.

After about ten minutes some of the soldiers seemed to become bored with having a blonde-haired Western woman in their midst, but I continued to find the atmosphere in the hut intimidating and oppressive. I was much relieved when Ahmed – the soldier who had escorted Dr Raad and myself into the hut – called from the door, '*Yalla* (Come on)!' indicating that I should follow him. It was a short walk, across a yard and into a three-storey concrete building. Ahmed led me into a room containing only a table and some chairs. He pointed to a box on the table which contained a grubby, crumpled winceyette night-dress. I certainly wasn't going to put that dirty rag on. I shook my head in what I hoped was a determined fashion. Ahmed lifted the barrel of his gun a little higher and pointed to the box again, as he did so issuing a barked instruction in Arabic that I didn't under-stand. I could see he was disturbed, but I was obdurate – winceyette, dirty or clean, no way. He seemed to realise there was no point pursuing it further: '*Malish* (No matter, never mind).'

He led me out, and we entered another room on the ground floor where I was greeted in English by a short, smiling Iraqi with a scar across his nose. He seemed friendly. 'Please sit down. I am an interpreter and this man,' he said, nodding towards the stern-faced, steely-eyed character behind the desk, 'would like you to answer some questions.'

The process of arriving at this meeting had been unnerving, but now I felt a sense of relief that at last I was going to find out what this business was all about. I sat down at a table next to the man who had introduced himself as the interpreter, opposite the one who wanted some answers from me. The room we were in was large and fairly comfortably decorated; it even had a sofa. In addition to the three of us there were another two men. Later these two would also question me and later still they would be replaced by another two and after that another two or three – each of whom would fire ques-tions at me via the interpreter. The way my interrogators would wander in and out of the room seemed, at first, very casual, but I soon realised that even when not in the room they must be able to listen in to everything that was said there, otherwise it would have been impossible for them to consistently pick up the line of questioning as they did.

The stern-faced man rapped out a short sentence in Arabic. Turning to me with a smile the interpreter asked politely, 'Could you tell us where you were last Monday and Tuesday?'

I thought for a moment. Today was Tuesday, what was I doing a week ago today? Suddenly a feeling of immense relief flooded through me. So, that was it! I couldn't help smiling.

'Last Monday and Tuesday I spent the day with a friend of mine, a British journalist. We drove to Hilla,' I told them. 'He had permission from the Ministry of Information to visit Hilla. They were going to send him a car, but it never showed up,' I added, just for good measure.

Although I was relieved that it was only the trip to Hilla which, after all, over a dozen or so British journalists had also made at that time, I couldn't help wondering what Farzad had been playing at. The last time I'd seen him, on Thursday, he had said that he'd be leaving Iraq the following day. I wondered if he might have written something controversial for the *Observer*, which would have been published in London two days later. The time-scale certainly would fit with my being brought here today, Tuesday. But if Farzad had written anything about our trip to Hilla, he had invented it. I had been there with him and it had been completely uneventful.

Anxious to get away, I described the events of our two trips to Hilla in detail. I had nothing to hide. I wasn't worried about anything other than getting back to work and, thinking they would send me off as soon as they had finished questioning me, my main feeling was one of 'For God's sake, get on with it. Let's get it over with and let me get out of here.'

I didn't think Farzad's scooping bits of dirt into containers could possibly amount to anything very much. At Hilla I actually felt at one time that he was behaving in a rather affected manner, hamming it up a bit for my benefit, the hotshot journalist on the trail of a scoop. I thought he was playing around with nothing more than a pile of ash or coal-dust, something completely insignificant. I wasn't watching him when he took the sample, although I was aware of him fairly carelessly throwing something into the glove compartment of the jeep when he returned to it. True, the last time I had seen him he had mentioned the containers, but he'd played the whole thing down, saying, 'It's not a problem, forget it.' Perhaps I should have realised, but I didn't. I just kept congratulating myself on the fact that there had been no wire-climbing, no attempt to do anything or see anything that in any way breached the rules.

So I told my story in detail, and then I told it again, and then again.

'Last Monday I packed a cool-box with drinks, checked over the car, collected Farzad from his hotel and drove to Hilla. We found a gate guarded by a soldier who spoke to us. We drove away. Farzad saw a pile of ashes at the roadside. We stopped; he looked; we left. On the way home we had tea at a tea-house. I dropped him back at his hotel before 2 p.m., when he was due at a press conference. That evening he telephoned me and asked if we could do the same the next day; I agreed. This time, Farzad took a little soil from the pile of ashes by the roadside and put them into a couple of containers I had given him.'

'How did you get to Hilla?'

'I followed the road signs.'

'What did you talk about on the journey?'

'We told jokes.'

'What sort of jokes?'

'Jokes, just silly jokes.'

'Political jokes?'

'No, knock-knock jokes, just silly jokes.'

'Who carried the cool-box when you left your flat?'

'Farzad.'

'Who told you the way to Hilla?'

'Nobody. I told you, we followed the road signs.'

'What did the soldier say to you?'

'He said "Good morning", and he told us we were one kilometre from the site of the explosion, but that we might as well go home since we would not be allowed to go in.'

33

'What was it that interested Bazoft at the roadside?'

'Nothing really, a pile of ashes, a heap of dust.'

'What did he say about it?'

'He said it might have come from the explosion.'

'How many times had you been to Hilla?'

'I have been there twice: once last Monday and once on Tuesday.'

'Had you ever been to Hilla before?'

'No.'

'Did Bazoft tell you the way to Hilla?'

'Yes. No. He knew vaguely where it was from his friends, from the other British journalists, but I found it by following the road signs. It is well signposted.'

'This was on Wednesday?'

'No, this was on Monday and Tuesday. I did not go to Hilla on Wednesday.'

On and on and on it went. The same questions put to me in different ways by different interrogators, some nice, some nasty, but always through the moderating voice of the interpreter. My head began to swim as I listened to the questions first in Arabic, which I couldn't understand, then in English. I gave my answer in English and back it would go in Arabic. The interrogators would change, but the questioning went relentlessly on.

After what seemed like hours – I had no way of knowing because my watch had been taken from me earlier – two men came into the room and asked me to sit on the sofa. Here was a change of tack: all these two were after was a friendly chat.

'You can trust us, it will be all right. Nothing bad is going to happen to you. Just tell us what happened, as it happened, and everything will be fine.'

After several minutes of reassurance from the good guys I returned to the table, where the last interrogator had been replaced by a fresh and more forceful bad guy than the last. He wasted no time.

'Right, in your own words, what exactly happened last Monday?'

I turned to the interpreter in exasperation. 'Look, we've

already been through all this. I've told you everything that happened, just as it happened, everything I know. I can't tell you any more. There is no more.'

The interrogator sneered and launched into a tirade in Arabic. The interpreter looked almost apologetic.

'There are just one or two more things that we still need to check out. Where did you get the containers you gave to Bazoft?'

'From the hospital.'

'How did they come to be in your apartment?'

'They were part of a damaged batch that arrived at the hospital. When a batch of sterile equipment is damaged in transit it is useless and either sent back or thrown away. I took the containers I gave Farzad from a damaged batch.'

'How many A-A guns did you see at Hilla?'

'I don't know what an A-A gun is.'

'How many A-A guns did Bazoft see at Hilla?'

'I don't know what an A-A gun looks like, but the only gun I saw, so the only gun Farzad could have seen, was an ordinary gun carried by the soldier on guard at the perimeter fence.'

'What sort of a gun was it?'

'I don't know, an ordinary gun, a rifle I suppose you would call it, the kind all soldiers in Baghdad carry with them.'

Between them they gave me little time to think, but in the back of my mind I was cursing Farzad. What the hell had he written in the Sunday papers? It must have been something bad, something they really hadn't liked if they felt they had to put me through this. At that point I believed he had really dropped me in it, and I resented it.

All this was going on in the back of my mind as I continued to answer the questions. It seemed that in order to get out of there it was up to me to emphasise that we hadn't seen anything, we hadn't done anything, we had remained on the outside of the fence and seen nothing of the actual explosion area. We had stayed within the law as far as I was concerned and anything that Farzad had written about or said he had seen must have been in his imagination.

35

I had not eaten since the morning, but food was the last thing on my mind. Now, in addition to questions on every conceivable aspect of the trips to Hilla, the interrogators launched into an investigation of my relationship with Farzad.

'How did you meet Bazoft?'

'He came to the Ibn Al Bitar hospital with two officials from the Ministry of Information.'

'Then what happened?'

'Farzad asked me some questions about the hospital. I told him what I could . . .'

'What did you tell him?'

'I told him what we did, how many patients we had, general information, nothing very much. Then I took him and the two Ministry of Information officials into the hospital restaurant, where we had tea.'

'And then he left the hospital?'

'Yes.'

'And you met him later?'

'Yes, he asked me, in front of the two officials, if he could telephone me. I told him he could, but I said I couldn't give him any more information about the hospital and suggested that if he needed anything more, he should contact Ibn Al Bitar's General Manager. I gave him the name and extension number.'

'Did he telephone the General Manager?'

'Yes.'

'Did he telephone you?'

'Yes, he phoned me later that day at the hospital and invited me to dinner.'

'What did you say?'

'I accepted his invitation.'

'Where did you go with him?'

'We just went to the restaurant at the Melia Hotel.'

'You went with him to his hotel?'

'Yes, we had dinner in the restaurant at his hotel.'

'Then what happened?'

'I went home.'

'After you had had dinner with him you went back to your apartment?'

'Yes.'

'Alone?'

'Yes.'

'What did you have for dinner?'

'Er, chicken, I think. Yes, chicken.'

The whole thing was becoming more and more bizarre. Their questions seemed – if possible – to have even less relevance than before. It was clear they were having difficulty with the fact I had agreed to have dinner with a man I hardly knew, and they went over each minute detail time and time again.

'Why did you agree to have dinner with Bazoft?'

'Well, he's British.'

Perhaps it didn't seem like a very convincing answer, but even as Iraqi nationals they must have had some idea of what life as an expatriate in Baghdad was like. We were foreigners away from home, and friendships were struck up almost instantaneously. I loved working in the Middle East and I had developed a real affection for the Arabs as a race – their culture and many of their customs. Yet I wouldn't want to have lived in isolation from other Europeans. After nearly a year in Iraq I had met most of the long-term expatriate community. They were generally good fun and I had made many friends: we had shared our own customs and our own culture. Inevitably, someone just arrived from Britain was much in demand, for they brought with them the latest gossip about Margaret Thatcher, the Channel Tunnel, the Test Match. To hear about these things at first hand was always fascinating.

Apart from being a new face, Farzad had a special quality that was difficult to pin down. He appeared to be quite unphased by anything life had thrown at him and he was such fun to be with – attentive, yet never in a way that was cloying, irreverent but not cruel, and always open to other points of view. He wasn't in Iraq to fend off the effects of the economic recession at home. He was here to work at a job he

37

enjoyed, and his enthusiasm for everything he did was an almost tangible and a very contagious thing. How did I begin to explain all this to my Iraqi interrogators?

'He is not British,' the interpreter said blankly. 'He is Iranian.' That threw me. I had never considered that Farzad might be anything other than British.

'Well, as far as I am concerned he's British. He told me he was British, he sounded British. He speaks perfect English.' I thought about Farzad's moderate public-school accent. 'He's clearly been to school in England,' I responded defensively.

'But you could see he wasn't British,' the interrogator snapped back via the interpreter.

Could I see he wasn't British? He was obviously not Anglo-Saxon British, that was clear from his name alone. His skin was a dark olive colour, and with his dark hair and dark eyes I suppose if I had asked myself what his origins were, I would have thought that one of his parents was probably Asian. Everything about Farzad seemed so very British – his accent, his behaviour, his demeanour – that I'd never entertained the possibility that he might be anything else. I had met many people – particularly working in hospitals and clinics – with dark skins and unusual names, who were just as British as I was. The British National Health Service would be hard-pressed to keep going without the many young Asian doctors and nurses it employs, a large percentage of whom were born in Britain.

I tried to point this out. 'In London there are thousands of people who are British. Even though they don't look British, they were born in Britain – Daley Thompson, for instance.'

They were clearly not convinced but moved back to the thorny question of why I agreed to have dinner with a man I didn't really know. I answered their questions automatically, but my mind was on conversations I had had with Farzad about his family. When we'd had dinner together in England I felt sure he'd told me his mother was Italian, but it's possible that I misheard him; perhaps he'd said 'Iranian'. He told me he had a brother in Scandinavia. I remembered that, but there had never been any mention of Iran as such, no conversations about visits there or relatives in the country.

I still was not unduly worried. Iraq's war with Iran was over before I arrived in the country; the cease-fire had been declared on the very day I'd signed the contract to go to the Ibn Al Bitar hospital. Although there were still a lot of soldiers with guns standing around the streets and public buildings, there was no sign of any conflict between Iran and Iraq at that time. However, I could see how much people had suffered during almost ten years of war. I knew there had been massive loss of life on both sides and I had been told the Iraqis had suffered shortages of everything, including the most basic foodstuffs – but now, although there were still shortages, there seemed to be a concerted effort among the people to put things back in order, to get on with the future rather than dwelling on the past.

The interrogation lasted for seven hours. I spotted the time from the interpreter's watch when he said he would accompany me upstairs. It was after 11 p.m. Every word that had been spoken during that time had been written down in Arabic and English. It still made no sense to me. Well, I had missed my shift. Someone else would have taken over the responsibility of being on the cardiac arrest team by now. I only hoped it hadn't been too inconvenient. I felt totally frazzled. I had never endured anything like the past seven hours before in my life and fervently hoped I never would again. I was light-headed as the lift stopped at the second floor.

The interpreter walked down a long corridor, banging shut the twenty or so hatch doors. I vaguely wondered why he was doing this; each slam jarred my nerves. Suddenly, realisation dawned. These were cells. We were walking down a corridor of cells. Dear God, they were going to lock me up! He unlocked a door about two-thirds of the way down the corridor and motioned me inside. The cell was completely empty except for a piece of foam mattress on the floor with two blankets folded on top. At the far end of the cell was a

39

sort of stable-type door. The interpreter looked through the open top half and grimaced.

'Here you will rest,' he told me. 'Someone will bring you breakfast in the morning.'

I was completely numb, too numb to object or even complain.

'May I keep the light on?' I croaked. 'I won't sleep tonight.'

'Nor me,' he said as he turned to leave.

He looked shocked at the squalid conditions in which I was to be left. It seemed that like me he was seeing the inside of a cell for the first time.

When I was alone I looked through the open stable-door into what passed as a washroom, and knew why the interpreter had grimaced. It was filthy. There was a foul lavatory bowl in the corner. A cold tap hung about a foot from the ground at the end of a length of leaking and rusty piping, but since I had no soap, towel or toothbrush I couldn't have used it even if I could have brought myself to touch it with bare hands. Hearing me, or sensing my presence, a dozen or so large cockroaches scurried into a drain in the floor. I shuddered. The morning couldn't come soon enough.

I spent the night sitting up, wide awake on the foam mattress. My mind was now quite clear. I thought back to the previous week and the trips with Farzad. We had done nothing wrong. We had driven around a perimeter fence. It was no different from driving around the roads of Greenham Common, and there was no law against that.

Every line of interrogation over the last seven hours seemed to lead back to the same basic points. What were you looking for at Hilla; what did you see? But surely I had answered those questions time and time again. For what must have been the three hundredth time that night I cast my mind back to Hilla. The picture remained the same. There had been nothing, just nothing to see. There was a wire fence, there were grass and trees and scrubby bushes – end of story. Again I thought about the pile of ash at the roadside and again dismissed it as insignificant. Whatever Farzad may have thought – and he did go on about the possibility of the ash being debris from the explosion – I couldn't believe it was so important, otherwise it surely wouldn't have been left on the roadside like that: it would have been kept inside the site. None of it made any kind of sense to me.

There was no natural light in the cell so I didn't see dawn breaking; I knew it was morning only when the hatch opened.

'*Sabah al here* (Good morning),' said the guard. I jumped up and ran to the door, but he just put a tick in the record book he was holding and moved on to the next hatch. I returned to my mattress. Minutes later there was a knock at the door and again I jumped up and looked out. The eyes of the tea-boy outside widened in disbelief when he saw a fair-haired, blue-eyed female staring back at him. He stood immobile, blinked once and stared again as his mouth opened and closed soundlessly.

'Hello!' I said in a friendly voice. That did it: leaving his trolley, he ran off down the corridor. I peered out of the hatch. A large tea-kettle stood on a metal trolley identical to the one used in the mortuary at the hospital. Beside the kettle stood a dirty yellow box filled with bread and next to that a large vat of something gooey and yellow. It didn't look very appetising to me, but that was an opinion clearly not shared by the cloud of flies that hovered and buzzed about it.

The tea-boy returned with a friend; now I had two of them gawping in at me.

'*Chi min fadlik* (I would like some tea, please)!' I said in my best Arabic. The second tea-boy held up a broken cup and pointed to the washroom. I remembered seeing a blue plastic cup on the floor beside the tap and went to fetch it. It was covered in sticky black slime and there was nothing to clean it with. I returned to the hatch.

'*Hallas* (It is finished),' I announced, improvising with one of the few Arabic words I knew.

'OK,' replied tea-boy number one. '*Shweya, shweya* (Hold on, hold on).' He gave me another cup that was marginally cleaner and filled it with hot, sweet black tea from the kettle. I prefer my tea white and without sugar as a rule, but this tasted like nectar. I was less sure about the bowl of sticky yellow liquid he scooped up from the fly-covered vat, but thought the bread would probably be all right.

'What is your name?' I asked in Arabic.

'Abdul Rahmed,' he replied. He pointed first at himself and then at me.

'Dee,' I answered.

'Tee?'

'No, Dee.'

'Hello, Tee.' He smiled at me and moved on.

The hours dragged endlessly by. Every time I heard a movement outside the cell I leapt to the hatch. Each time a guard passed I pointed to his watch and he would show me the time. I waited all day for someone to come and release me. Surely it could only be a matter of sitting it out for another hour or two.

My early feelings of optimism gave way to anger and eventually to despair as the day wore on. Had Dr Raad kept his word and telephoned the British Embassy to tell them where I had been taken? What if he had been warned to say nothing, then what would he do? I didn't want to dwell on this point, but kept returning to it. If Dr Raad hadn't told anyone, there seemed little hope of the Iraqis letting me go until they were good and ready. Surely if he had contacted the Embassy somebody would have come to get me by now. What about Michelle? What about my family? How would they get to know where I was unless the Embassy had been told? Anguished thoughts ricocheted around my head until I was unable to think straight. I remonstrated with myself: 'For God's sake, get a grip on it!' For a while this would calm me down until something else, some other horrible scenario I hadn't before contemplated, popped unbidden into my head and I was back where I started, in a state of even greater anguish and turmoil.

A trolley came around carrying rice and some sort of meat stew in large open vats. The ever-present crowd of flies hung above it and settled on the meat each time the trolley stopped at a hatch door. I saw the arm of my next-door neighbour holding out a bowl and heard him speaking in Arabic. How many of us are here, I wondered, and what for? How long do people stay? Are there any other women, or other Westerners?

The food looked disgusting, but I was beyond caring. I couldn't remember when I had last eaten a meal. The yellow goo at breakfast was, I discovered, some sort of lentil soup and completely inedible, resembling wallpaper adhesive as much as anything else. Lunch had been a thick macaroni-style soup that I had found only slightly more palatable, but by now chronic hunger pangs had made me less choosy.

After dinner I lay down on my mattress and fell into a troubled sleep. I wakened some hours later with a terrible headache, nausea and stomach cramps. I knew immediately what it was – gastro-enteritis. I stumbled to the filthy wash-room, barely noticing the frenetic activity my appearance heralded among the cockroach population. Falling to my knees I heaved the contents of my stomach into the disgusting lavatory bowl, then grasping it for support, stood up and turned around to deal with a violent attack of diarrhoea. Much later I crawled back across the filthy floor to my mattress and wept as I hadn't since I was a child.

Solitary

For three long days the sickness and diarrhoea continued, although the initial intensity of the attacks diminished. Nobody had yet been to see me and I was becoming concerned that if three days could go by without me being missed, I was well on the way to becoming the subject of one of those expatriate stories about women who disappear into the desert never to be heard of again. What had they told my colleagues at the hospital? Where did my friends think I was? What in Heaven's name had they said to Michelle?

I decided to exploit my physical condition. The guards could not have failed to hear me careering around the cell for the last three days, in a desperate attempt to reach the washroom before I vomited – or worse – on my mattress. I would ask for a doctor. If I could see a doctor, it would almost certainly be someone who could speak English and perhaps he or she would be able to help me. I waited for a guard to pass by.

'Excuse me. Doctor, *min fadlik*, please.'

The guard peered at me through the hatch in the cell door before going away and returning with another guard I had not seen before.

'You have problem? You want doctor?'

'Oh, thank God, you can speak English. What's your name?'

'My name is Hamid. I learned to speak English at school. What is the problem?'

'I am sick, Hamid. I have been very sick for three days. Can you find me a doctor who speaks English?'

'*Shweya, shweya,*' he told me, pressing together the thumb and first two fingertips of his right hand. After delivering the eternal Arabic plea to wait and be patient, he disappeared.

Sometime later Hamid returned, took a set of keys from his belt and motioned me to come out of the cell. I did so hesitantly, half-elated to be getting out of this tiny hell-hole for however short a time, yet half-afraid of what I would find on the other side of the metal door.

'Cover your eyes,' he said, handing me a crude blindfold made of some sort of dirty sacking material and covered on the outside with shiny PVC. I pulled it over my eyes. Hamid took my arm and led me, stumbling from a combination of disorientation and weakness from three days without food, along the corridor to the lift. We descended, to what I now know was the ground floor, where I was ushered through a maze of corridors. We stopped outside a door on which he tapped lightly.

'You come, please,' Hamid instructed.

After helping me shuffle to a chair, where I sat down, I heard him turn and leave the room. The door closed. The room was completely silent, but I felt there was someone in there with me. Was the doctor watching me? It was an unnerving feeling; my stomach was in knots.

'Take off your blindfold,' a man's voice commanded.

I pulled it over my head and gasped. The room was full of men, and they didn't look like doctors. They were seated on chairs and sofas, on the arms of the furniture and lined up two or three deep towards the back of the large room in which I found myself. There must be at least twenty-five men here, I thought in bewilderment. What on earth was all this about? What could I have done that could possibly warrant such intense interest from so many people, all of whom, judging by their appearance and the cut of their Western-style clothes, held positions of some importance in this place?

45

'Good morning!' The greeting came out from a sea of faces. I looked towards the voice, but there were so many of them it was difficult to pinpoint exactly who had spoken. I said 'Good morning', but to no one in particular.

'I am your interpreter. My name is Abu Samir.' It was the same voice as before, but it was not the interpreter I had spoken to when I first arrived from the hospital. The first interpreter, the one with a scar across his nose, had been quite friendly. There was no sign of friendliness on this man's face. He was tall, with an athletic build, pale skin and a round face. Handsome but hostile. They all looked hostile.

'We would like you to answer some questions,' the interpreter barked at me harshly. I was still in a state of shock at seeing this huge number of men in a room where I had hoped to find only an English-speaking doctor. Their faces glared at me now, each one the very picture of a hard-faced, hard-nosed interrogator. I was scared.

It must have been fear that made me attack first. 'Why have I been left lying in a cell for three days?' I demanded loudly of everyone in the room.

I sat before them absolutely filthy after spending three days in a disgusting cell. My nails were caked with dirt, my hair was matted. The white blouse and green skirt of the nursing officer's uniform I had been wearing when I was brought here were now stained, stinking and vomit-splattered. They stared at me as if I was a zoo animal, each with his well-pressed trousers, clean shirt and neatly-brushed hair. I was outraged.

'I have been unable to wash, clean my teeth, brush my hair,' I protested. 'It's a matter of everyday hygiene. Look at me. Is this how you treat people here?'

An astonished silence descended on the room. There had been a general buzz of conversation after I had removed my blindfold, but this outburst caused complete surprise. The men looked at me and at each other. Then the interrogator who had introduced himself as Abu Samir gave me a sardonic smile and said, 'You look beautiful.'

The room rocked with laughter. Although the joke was on me, I laughed too. The atmosphere was somehow broken by the laughter, and I was beginning to feel a little light relief. Perhaps it would be all right. But my optimism was short-lived.

'You are a spy!' shrieked a voice very close to me. I turned to look at my accuser. He put his face up close to mine. 'You are a spy!' He spat out the words at me. I could feel the heat of his breath on my face and the smell of his mouth as he snarled at me.

'No,' I said calmly.

'Yes!'

'No.'

'Yes, yes, yes!' He screamed even louder.

I shifted my body back in the chair away from him. 'No,' I said very quietly. He moved away.

I turned back to the interpreter, Abu Samir, and said, in what I hoped sounded a reasonable voice, 'I'm not a spy, I never have been a spy and I have no wish to be one. Right now I have gastro-enteritis and I really believe I might die if I stay in these conditions.'

'Good!' Abu Samir spoke directly to me, a nasty smile cracking his face. 'That is what we hope – that you will die. We do not like spies.'

I felt sick and faint. This was worse than my worst nightmares. This was no longer about an innocent trip to Hilla with Farzad: it was something much more serious than that. I remembered a colleague at the Ibn Al Bitar hospital who, after a few drinks, had crashed his car into a stationary train. He had been thrown into jail for three days and then released. In the back of my mind, I realised that this is what I thought would happen. I had considered very little aside from the discomfort of being dishevelled and dirty and the embarrassment of having to return to the hospital and tell my colleagues I had been thrown in an Iraqi jail for a few days for getting into a spot of bother with the authorities. Now, this man was yelling that he hoped I would die and, looking at his twisted features, I could easily believe him. Sweat broke out on my face, my heart was beating much too fast, I began to feel lightheaded, my blood pressure must be dropping . . .

When I came round I was back in my cell, lying on the mattress. Had I passed out? I remembered someone yelling 'You are a spy!' They obviously wanted me dead and who was I to stand up against the might of the Iraqi establishment? They had decided I was guilty and since I had heard nothing from the British Embassy, I must assume they agreed – after all, they seemed to be able to get football hooligans home within twenty-four hours. But what about my family? They must have realised something was amiss by now.

I wondered again what Michelle had been told and how she would cope. I couldn't even begin to imagine, but I knew that somehow she would. She was twenty-one, fun-loving, a bit irresponsible at times perhaps, but then who was I to talk? It wasn't Michelle who was banged up in an Iraqi jail. All the warnings I had given her over the years came back to me: be careful, be cautious, be on your guard. All the nights I had wondered and worried where she might be and what she might be up to. Every time she had come up trumps, phoning me, albeit often long past midnight, to let me know where she was and when she would be back; introducing me to her friends so that I knew who she was with and where she could be contacted. Now our positions were reversed, but there was no way I could let her know where I was or who I was with to put her mind at rest. Thinking about Michelle and the certain knowledge she would be able to cope with whatever was thrown at her cheered me up no end and strengthened my flagging resolve. No one was going to kill me off. I would fight all the way. I was going to get out of here, somehow. I had my children to consider. But to achieve my objectives I would have to work on my physical and mental fitness. I stood up and reached towards the ceiling, then bent over to touch my toes. I brought a foot up behind my back, caught it with my hand and leaned forward as I had seen footballers doing before a match.

I looked up when I heard a stifled giggle. Guards crowded around the hatch in my cell door.

'What you do? You crazy!' one of them said.

I smiled at him and carried on. I sang 'Tiptoe through the

Tulips' softly to myself as I walked around the seven paces by four, and that included the mattress, of my stone cell. I discovered that by walking in a figure of eight I could make the walk last even longer, and this also seemed to have the effect of preventing giddiness.

I sat down on the mattress and practised deep-breathing exercises, yoga-style, sitting in the lotus position, pretending in turn to be a lion, a kitten, a cow. If exercising my body and my imagination was the key to getting through this, then I would get through it. The Iraqis might have thought they were dealing with a weak and feeble English woman but I knew I was made of sterner stuff.

There was a knock at the door. The tea-boy stood there with an Arabic newspaper. I shook my head sadly. I would have enjoyed reading a newspaper, even one full of political propaganda, as I knew the ones published in Iraq had to be to pass the censor, but I couldn't read Arabic.

'*Macko Arabee* (No Arabic),' I told him.

He continued to beckon me over to the door, pointing at something. I saw it was a photograph of Margaret Thatcher in a particularly unflattering pose. Who cared! It was something from home. I took the newspaper and carefully tore out the picture. Folding over the top, I hung it on the washroom step and screwed up the rest of the paper to make a ball. It was too light, so I wet it, compressed it into a round shape and left it to dry. Tomorrow, I thought to myself, I will have it bouncing around the walls.

During those first few days in the interrogation centre my spirits rose and fell almost by the hour. I tried to rationalise my position. Since I hadn't done anything, it could only be a matter of time before I was released. Yet I had told them all I knew, so why was I still here?

They had taken my watch away when I was arrested, so that without the arrival of the food-trolley at mealtimes I would have had no idea whether it was night or day. Every day was the same, up with the early-morning tea-trolley and to bed after the evening meal. The only days that were different were the ones when I was taken from my cell to answer questions.

'You are a liar, like all Jews!' screamed the interrogator as I walked blindfold into the interrogation room.

'No,' I replied. 'And besides, I'm not Jewish.'

'But would you agree that all Jews are liars?' he shouted as he yanked off my blindfold.

'I wouldn't know,' I replied, as calmly as I was able. 'When am I going to see the Consul from the British Embassy?'

'You will not see the Consul. You are a spy.'

'I am not a spy, but if I am not to be allowed to see the Consul, may I request a food box from the Red Cross?'

'No, the Red Cross is not here.'

'You are mistaken.' I smiled up at him. 'There is a team from the Red Cross in Baghdad. I have seen and spoken to the Team Leader.'

'What is the Leader's name?'

'Doctor Joseph.'

'Is he Jewish?'

'I have no idea; whether or not he is Jewish doesn't interest me.'

'How many Jewish friends do you have in London?'

'I don't know. In London no one is interested in the religion of other people, at least no one I know. My friends could be Buddhist, Hindu, Muslim, Jewish or Roman Catholic, or anything else come to that. I have never thought to ask.'

'You are a liar. Go back to your cell.'

So back to my cell I went, until the next time. I had been here for ten days and, so far, there had been nothing to indicate that anyone on the outside, other than Dr Raad, was aware of my plight. The interrogations continued. The accusations were always the same: I was a spy, a liar, a Jew.

From my early dislike I had developed a healthy hatred of the interpreter Abu Samir. An interpreter's job, I felt, should be to translate one language into another. He was there to tell me, in English, what the interrogators had said in Arabic. Abu Samir, however, took on the role of interpreter/interrogator. It seemed to me he enjoyed his job too much. All the harassment and intimidation meted out by the interrogators were far more in his line than simple translation. Perhaps he was looking for promotion.

It would be wrong to say I enjoyed interrogation, but dreadful as those two or three sessions a week were, they broke the monotony of my life in solitary confinement. Without them the only events were the visits of the tea-boy, who also gave me the occasional paper, and mealtimes, when the trolley would stop outside my cell door to dispense its load of instant salmonella.

The days were turning into weeks. I had begun keeping a record: every night I would scratch a single stroke in the filthy paintwork of the washroom door. In the outside world it was October. I had been arrested on Tuesday 19 September – surely my family must be aware by now that something had happened to me?

One day I was digging into the plaster around the water tap with my fingernails in the hope of gouging out sufficient plaster to allow me a peephole to the outside world, when I heard a key turn in my cell door. Ahmed, the tall young guard who was on duty the afternoon of my arrest, stood in the doorway, holding out a blindfold. He escorted me on the by now familiar walk downstairs, and I was left outside the interrogation room, facing the wall.

Voices floated along the corridor. I had discovered that by leaning the top half of my body back from the waist I could sometimes peep out from beneath the blindfold. I tipped back my head and surprise, surprise, spotted a face from the past. It was Abdullah, the guard from the Ibn Al Bitar hospital, who wore brown shoes instead of the regulation black and because of it was rumoured to be an official informer to the Iraqi authorities. I had discounted the rumours then, putting them down to what I believed was a general Iraqi obsession with conspiracy theories. I didn't have time to reflect on the fact that hindsight always seems to offer the best view of a situation. I was too pleased to see a familiar face.

'Hello Abdullah!' I called out joyously.

His face froze. 'Turn your face to the wall,' he yelled as he hurried away. Clearly the rumours at the hospital had been true – Abdullah was an informer. I turned back towards the wall, sick with disappointment.

I thought I had spotted a friend. Abdullah had spent a lot of time around the Ibn Al Bitar hospital and although it was rumoured he was only there to spy on us, he and I had exchanged pleasantries. Even so I felt a fool. Of course he wasn't going to greet me like a long-lost friend: as an employee of the Iraqi regime how could he be anything other than my enemy? Six weeks in this place had obviously impaired my judgement. If I started to believe all that was familiar was also friendly, I would really be in serious trouble.

The dreaded Abu Samir came out of the interrogation room. I knew it was him because of the way he manhandled me through the door and on to a chair. He yanked off my blindfold. An interrogator sat behind the desk. His pale skin, brown hair and hazel eyes gave him a European appearance, but there was something strangely lopsided about him which I couldn't at first work out. After a few moments I realised that the two sides of his face were quite different; nothing seemed to balance. One eye was very slightly higher than the other, as was one of his nostrils and one side of his mouth. He was flanked by another interrogator who looked like a demented garden gnome. The Gnome was dark-skinned, with deep-brown eyes and a wide, cruel, almost lunatic grin. The Gnome picked up a pile of files and threw them down on the desk in front of me.

'These files contain a record of the numerous occasions you visited the American Embassy,' Abu Samir translated. 'You were followed and photographed with the people you met there.'

I laughed. 'That's impossible. I have never been to the American Embassy.'

'But you know people who work there.'

'Yes, I've met several diplomats. One tends to meet most of the expatriates working in Baghdad at some time or another.'

'What are their names?'

I named an American diplomat I had been introduced to and met on a number of occasions socially.

'He is a spy.'

'Well, if he's a spy, it's certainly news to me.'

'Who do you know from the British Embassy?'

'Robin Kealy, the First Secretary and Pauline Waugh, the Consul. I have shaken hands with the Ambassador and there is one other person I met at a party given by an Egyptian diplomat.' I named him.

'He, too, is a spy, an enemy of Iraq. As soon as we prove it, he will be sent home. Is he the person who sent you to the explosion site with Bazoft?'

'No, of course not. I have told you a thousand times, I went to Hilla of my own accord.'

He leaned forward in his chair and looked intently into my eyes. 'We know that you were sent there by either a British diplomat or an American diplomat. Which one was it?'

'Neither.'

The European-looking interrogator with the lopsided face got off his chair, walked around the desk and stood behind me. His very presence was intimidating. He reached out and pulled my hair, hard. Abu Samir moved his chair in front of the closed door. The Gnome moved to the other side of me; he was clearly enjoying himself. He kicked my leg. Lopsided pulled at my hair again on the other side of me. The Gnome kicked harder.

Kick. Kick.

Pull. Pull.

I took a deep breath and tried to keep my voice even.

'No one sent me to Hilla. I went of my own accord.'

Lopsided moved to the desk and picked up a brass knife with a long, pointed blade.

'Put on your blindfold,' he snarled.

With shaking hands, I put the blindfold over my head to cover my eyes. I was terrified. They were going to cut me and they had told me to put the blindfold on so that I wouldn't be able to identify which one of them did it. It would be their word against mine. Where would they cut me first – my face, my body, my throat?

My hands were cold and clammy as I unclenched them and tried to speak in a reasonable way.

'It was my idea to drive Farzad to the explosion site. He was keen to get a story for his newspaper. I was just giving him a lift because he's a friend of mine. He had permission from the Ministry of Information to visit the site, but the car didn't arrive. I have explained this a thousand . . .' My voice tailed off.

'We do not believe you. Take off your blindfold.'

I pulled it off with relief. There was no longer any sign of the knife, but the Gnome held a length of rubber hosepipe in his hand.

'We will beat you and smash you against the wall unless you confess that you work for the British Government.'

'I do not work for the British Government. I am a nursing officer, nothing more. That is the truth.' My head was pounding and I could feel rivulets of sweat running down my body. This was the first sign of physical violence to emerge at the interrogations. I was trying to pull myself together and maintain a calm exterior, but I know I was visibly shaking.

Suddenly, they changed tack. 'Look, all you have to do is say that the man you met at the Egyptian's party, the British diplomat, told you to go to the explosion site. Nothing will happen to him. He has diplomatic immunity and he will be sent home; then you will be able to leave.'

It was tempting. The social life of the Embassy staff in Baghdad was severely restricted, particularly since they had to seek written permission from the Iraqi authorities if they wanted to venture outside the city. Two or more years of meeting the same people at the same parties was monotonous and frustrating. The British diplomat would probably be delighted to be sent home, I thought. However, common sense prevailed. It would be stupid to lie. I hadn't so far and some seventh sense told me this would be the wrong time to start.

'I'm sorry, I can't say that. It's not true.'

The interrogators rose and silently left the room. Only Abu

Samir remained, his malicious smile still in place. Now that the danger had passed I was filled with fury at this smirking, vicious bully.

'I am memorising your face,' I told him. 'When I get back to England, I'll make up an Identikit and have your face shown on television around the world.'

'No problem.' His smile grew wider. 'I'll give you a photograph if you like.'

'No thank you. I wouldn't want to look at such an ugly picture. In fact, I don't want to be in the same room with you. I'm going back to my cell.' I turned, ran out of the room, along the corridor, into the lift and up to the third floor where Ahmed, the young guard, was waiting. Taking my arm he put me back into the lift, but instead of going back down to the interrogation room, we stopped at the second floor where Ahmed handed me over to another guard, one I didn't know. He swiftly dispatched me to the cooler.

The cooler was a dark, claustrophobic room with a broken lavatory at one end, so it was back to using the drain in the floor. The hatch was kept shut. Were they going to starve me out, I wondered? I remained in this dungeon for eighteen hours. To stay sane I sang songs from musicals, nursery rhymes and songs dating back to my teenage years.

> Once I had a secret love
> That lived within the heart of me.
> All too soon my secret love
> Became impatient to be free.

I clapped my hands over my mouth in horror. My God, if the interrogators had bugged the cooler, they would think I was referring to secret things like espionage! Better change tack.

> I wanna go home,
> I wanna go home,
> I feel so broke up,
> I wanna go home.

Only months later did I consider how institutionalised I had already become. When I'd escaped from Abu Samir, who had made no attempt to follow me, I had run to the lift and headed back to my solitary cell on the third floor. The woman arrested weeks before would have headed for the ground floor and a dash for freedom. It didn't even occur to me to try.

Putting on the Pressure

I had been in solitary confinement for seven weeks, and I was still far from healthy because of the appalling diet and conditions. However, I was determined to keep my body in shape, even if mentally I was feeling evermore constricted by my circumstances, and exercise formed an important part of my daily ritual. But this late October day was not a day for aerobics or yoga. Pulling up the tail of my shirt, I wiped the sweat from my face. The air-conditioning had broken down and the temperature was well over a hundred degrees Fahrenheit. I lay back on my mattress dreaming of cold drinks and the coolness of Derwent Water, a wonderful, tranquil place where I had enjoyed a refreshing swim during a holiday in the English Lake District a few years ago.

A tap on the hatch door of my cell broke my reverie. The tea-boy stood outside waving a copy of the English-language *Baghdad Observer*. I accepted it eagerly. To anyone familiar with the newspaper it is no doubt incredible that its arrival filled me with such joy. I knew I was reading Iraqi political propaganda, but at least it was current propaganda. I read every word, the intense heat forgotten as I carefully tore out a picture of Andrew Lloyd Webber and placed him beside Mrs Thatcher on the washroom step. And now I could make another paper ball. I had been devastated when the first one had finally disintegrated, but now I could begin the whole soaking and shaping process again.

As I began to work with the paper my mind wandered.

What could have happened to Hamid, I asked myself? I had not seen the cheerful, English-speaking guard for several weeks and the loneliness of being surrounded by people who were unable to communicate with me was becoming almost impossible to bear.

As if on cue, I heard someone opening my cell door. It was Ahmed. He held out a blindfold: it looked as if I would soon have someone to speak English to. He led me down to the interrogation room. Inside, Abu Samir was already seated.

'Take off your blindfold and sit down.'

A wooden chair was placed in the centre of the room, whilst soft, upholstered armchairs and a television set lined the walls. I sat down on the wooden chair and looked towards Abu Samir, who was wearing his usual stony-faced expression.

The room filled up with interrogators, who sat talking amongst themselves. When the Chief Interrogator entered, everyone stood up. He went directly to the television set and turned it on. It was an Iraqi football match. All the interrogators turned to watch. Curiouser and curiouser. After a few minutes of this the interpreter spoke.

'You will see your friend Bazoft on TV in a few minutes.'

I was astonished. Farzad on television, here! What on earth was this all about?

'Where is he speaking from?' I asked.

'From Iraq.'

'Are you saying Farzad is back in Iraq now?'

'He never left Iraq. He is here with you in this prison.'

By now my mind was reeling as a dozen possibilities raced through it. I thought Farzad had left Baghdad weeks ago, just before my arrest. It was obviously a trick. They were telling me Farzad was in Iraq to get me to make some sort of trumped-up confession.

'I don't believe it, you are making it up,' I challenged Abu Samir.

'We will show him to you. Will that convince you? But you will not speak. If we show him to you, you must promise not to speak. Do you agree?'

'Yes,' I croaked, nodding my head. 'I promise I won't speak.'

Abu Samir gave an instruction to one of the other men, who immediately left the room. I sat back in my chair like someone suffering from shell-shock. My body was tense and I could feel the blood pounding in my head, but was unable to formulate a single thought. Seconds, or was it minutes later, the door of the interrogation room was thrown open and there in the doorway, wearing a pair of brown-and-white-striped pyjamas, stood Farzad. He was blindfold.

I gasped to see how thin he was, but it was him, unmistakably. His hair, his mouth, his hands, the way he stood, I was in no doubt, this wasn't a trick. Farzad was here in prison, but still it made no sense. I stared at his thin frame in the baggy prison-issue pyjamas and remembered how, only a few short weeks ago, he had looked so healthy and handsome in blue jeans and a pale-blue shirt as we set off for Hilla. As I continued to stare he was bundled away, looking more like a broken old man than the witty, vital friend with whom I had enjoyed so much laughter and good conversation.

As Farzad left the room, the Iraqi football match was switched off and a video cartridge was loaded into the machine. Suddenly, Farzad's face filled the screen. Beneath his eyes there were deep, black shadows as he stared vacantly out of the set. I had never seen Farzad looking like this; he must have suffered dreadfully, I thought. But as he began to speak, his words seemed to contradict my impressions.

'The treatment I have received,' he gulped, blinking his eyes rapidly, 'is much better than I would receive in a detention centre or institution in the UK.' He went on: 'In 1983 I got to know some Israeli intelligence officers as friends and in 1987 I was recruited by Israeli intelligence agents living in the United Kingdom under different covers.'

I listened in horror as his confession continued. He began to talk about the ill-fated trip to the explosion site at Hilla, referring to me as 'my girlfriend, Daphne Ann Parish'. Strange, I thought. How does he know my name is Daphne? He had never known me as anything other than Dee and he would certainly not have known my second name was Ann unless someone had told him. And as for referring to me as his girlfriend! I began to feel uneasy. There was no reason Farzad would say the things he was saying unless he had been forced to make a speech written by the interrogators. It was the only explanation.

The men in the room stared at me as I watched the rest of the twenty-minute video. They were clearly hoping for some outward sign of the stress I was feeling, but I was determined not to crack.

'Well,' said the interpreter after the video had finished and the television set had been switched off, 'What do you think of it?'

'Not very much,' I responded in a deadpan way, though my stomach was churning.

'Was Farzad telling the truth?'

'I wouldn't have thought so.'

'He is an Israeli spy. You heard him say so on the video. If you also confess to being a spy, seventeen million Iraqi people will forgive you and you will be allowed to go home.'

'I am not a spy.'

'We will send you back to the hospital tonight. We promise you this. Give us the information and you will be free by tonight.'

'What sort of information?'

'That you are a spy. That you work for the British Government. That you gave information to the Embassy here in Iraq to pass on to your country. Tell us everything and we will release you. Don't you want to go back to the hospital?'

Did I want to go back to the hospital? Was this man Abu Samir completely crazy? I was spending most of my time trying to think of a way to get out of this place. I had heard nothing from the hospital authorities, nothing from the British Embassy, nothing from Michelle, Martina or any of my family. I was confused and more than a little afraid that I had been completely forgotten in here. Did I want to go back to the hospital, he asked!

'Yes, of course I do,' I said quietly.

'We understand that you love your country, that you want to help it in any way you can.' His voice was cajoling now. 'We, too, would do the same for Iraq. Patriotism is no disgrace. But before we release you, you must tell the Iraqi people about what you have done. This is what we require in exchange for our forgiveness. Admit that you are a spy. Tell the Iraqi people what you have done and we will release you.'

Could it be that simple – just say I'm a spy and they will let me go? Well, that is certainly what they are saying. Perhaps it is true. I didn't believe them when they said Farzad was in Iraq, but he is and I have seen him. He had made a confession on video, so perhaps he is about to be released. Maybe they are telling the truth and it's a chance I have to take – what is the alternative?

I argued silently with myself. If I said I was a spy, there was a chance I would be released. If I told the truth, as I had been doing since I arrived here, I didn't seem to get much in return. Eventually I was poised to do it – to 'confess' to their ludicrous charges, but something stopped me. A phoney confession was on the tip of my tongue when I heard myself announce determinedly: 'I am not a spy. I do not work for the British Government. I am a nursing officer at the Ibn Al Bitar hospital and I am guilty only of giving a friend a lift in my car.'

It was not the answer they had been hoping for, but knowing what I now do, it probably saved my life.

The interrogation continued for hours. Questions were fired at me from every corner of the room. All of them could speak English, but at times preferred to work through the interpreter, Abu Samir. It was midnight when I was returned to my cell, their sneers still visible in my mind's eye and their insistent accusations – 'Liar, liar, spy!' – ringing in my ears.

The next morning a rumble of discontent passed along the corridor. The guard I had nicknamed 'Bad News' was on duty. Today all the prisoners would suffer. Bad News enjoyed exercising his authority to the full – we always knew when he was around because of all the shouting and banging of doors.

The medics would be called in to drag screaming prisoners from their cells to be held down by Bad News for intravenous injections of Valium to keep them quiet.

I went up to the hatch door, reached out and gently pulled it towards me until the catch softly clicked shut. But I had not been quiet enough; Bad News must have heard the click, and was striding the few steps to my cell. He wrenched the hatch door open and thrust his angry face through the opening.

'Sit!' he screamed at me viciously, his anger quite out of proportion to my supposed sin.

I sat down on the mattress and barked, 'Woof, woof!'

There goes a man looking at a heart attack, I thought, as his puce-coloured face disappeared from view. He moved on to the cell next door where he began ranting and raving at the unfortunate occupant. I eased myself off the mattress and crept back to the hatch door, where I could see him through the crack of the hinge, yelling in Arabic and waving his hands about maniacally. The argument seemed to be something to do with a blanket. Perhaps my neighbour had committed the same crime as I had a few weeks before when, for want of something better to do, I had picked bits of fluff off my blanket and heaped them up on the floor.

There was an almighty crash as Bad News slammed my neighbour's hatch door closed. From next door I could hear my neighbour pacing up and down his cell; even his footsteps sounded agitated. Then he moved into the washroom and turned on the tap. All day long the precious water, so revered in Iraq as in every desert country, splashed down the drain. Perhaps it was my neighbour's way of coping with his anger, perhaps the sound of the running water acted as some sort of therapy, but as far as the rest of us in the block were concerned he couldn't have chosen a worse way to vent his spleen. We were without water to wash in or to drink for twenty-two hours.

I was tearing up paper to make a papier-mâché chess set when I heard the last trickle of water go down my neighbour's drain. Damn, damn! Why hadn't I anticipated that the water would run out? I jumped up the step into my washroom, held my cup under the tap and turned it on. There was barely half a cupful.

I wasn't going to waste it on the chess set, so I turned my attention to other possible ways of using my time. There was always the Scrabble set, a screw of paper containing capital letters torn from headlines in the *Baghdad Observer*, but it would be difficult to play without a board. So, why not make one? But how? There was no paper or water left to mould a papier-mâché board. Perhaps I could scratch one into the stone floor of my cell. I roamed around the cell looking for a loose stone and found one in the wall by the tap in the washroom. My nails split and broke off as I attempted to prise it from the wall; it was not as loose as I had thought, but eventually it came away. I tried it – perfect. Now, how many squares are there on a Scrabble board? And where are the double- and triple-word score squares?

I decided to make the board fifteen squares by fifteen squares and painstakingly scratched this out on the stone floor. It didn't look right, but I had no way of correcting it. I should have scratched it lightly until it was perfect and then gone over it again with deeper scratches. Should I make another one? No, it had to be up here in the corner where the guards couldn't see it, otherwise they would send in the cleaners to erase it, as they had the calendar I had scratched out with my fingernail on the filthy paintwork of my wash-room door.

Imperfect as it was, it served a purpose. I picked out a letter for myself and one for my imaginary friend. Which friend? I decided on Joy, my Scrabble partner in England for almost twenty years. I wouldn't cheat Joy, would I?

I was back in the interrogation room. These sessions usually took place about two or three times a week and, it seemed, completely randomly. Sometimes I would be taken down in the morning and kept for only half an hour or forty minutes. At other times I would be taken down in the evening and questioned for several hours. The questions were always basically the same: why did I go to Hilla, who sent me there and what did I do, say or see there. However, since I had been allowed to see Farzad and to watch his video-taped confession a week ago, I had noticed a subtle change of tactics. All the interrogators' comments seemed to imply that since Farzad had admitted he was guilty, it could only be sheer bloody-mindedness that prevented me doing the same. They made no secret of the fact they were losing patience with me.

The two beauties who had earlier pulled my hair and kicked me, Lopsided and the Gnome, were sitting on a sofa. Abu Samir, the interpreter who had grinned as he watched them do it, stood at the other end of the room. Now what? I wondered, with a quiver of fear. The last time I had been in here the interrogators had almost badgered a 'confession' out of me. Since then I had had time to reflect, and I reckoned that as long as I continued to tell the truth, I would remain safe. But now, looking at the determined faces of these three brutes, I began to doubt my earlier resolve. Had they been sent in to beat a 'confession' out of me because others, using less physical methods, had failed?

As he stood blindfold in the doorway, Farzad had looked broken and defeated. After being returned to my cell I had wondered for hours about what treatment might have been meted out to him. Had he been beaten or tortured? I was aware of the often brutal treatment suffered by Iraqis who got in the way of even minor officialdom. It was not unusual to see an Iraqi policeman on traffic duty cuffing a youth or young man about the head for some minor misdemeanour, real or imagined. What then might a male prisoner under interrogation expect? After all, I had been fairly certain that being a foreigner and a woman would protect me from physical abuse, but these three had shown me otherwise.

'Sit down,' ordered Abu Samir, indicating a wooden chair placed in the centre of the room. I sat down without taking my eyes away from his face. The others, Lopsided and the Gnome, were the ones who had actually hurt me, but this bastard had sat with his chair against the door, grinning as they did it. He had enjoyed every minute of my fear and pain and I hated him for it.

He stared at me and said: 'Today you will meet your friend Farzad, but you must not speak to him. OK, do you agree?'

I nodded my head. I had thought about little else but Farzad since being allowed to see him last week. Why had he made that video? Had he been tortured? Was it possible that he was a spy? This last question caused me real torment. As far as I was concerned spies were something found between the pages of books by Ian Fleming and Hammond Innes. I thought of conversations I had had with Farzad: had there been any pointers there? I knew him as a young and ambitious man, who undoubtedly considered himself rather suave and sophisticated. But although his manners were impeccable, it would take more than that to make him some sort of James Bond. He loved to chat and one of his favourite topics of conversation was himself, not in an overbearing or arrogant way, but he enjoyed talking about his work, his friends, the people he worked with and the things he wanted to achieve. He would have been the worst possible material for a spy. If he'd been involved in anything in the least bit clandestine, I don't believe he could have stopped himself from blabbing about it.

I didn't know what this meeting, engineered by Abu Samir, was supposed to achieve, but I was more than happy for it to take place. Quite apart from being a friendly face, maybe Farzad would be able to throw some light on exactly what was going on.

The door was thrown open as Farzad was led into the room and pushed down into one of the comfortable armchairs opposite me. There was a glass-topped coffee table between us.

'Take off your blindfold,' instructed Abu Samir.

Farzad blinked a couple of times as his eyes adjusted to the light, then his face split into a wide grin. Despite the weight loss and the unhealthy pallor, he looked wonderful to me.

'Hello, Dee.'

'Hello, Farzad,' I replied and we both laughed.

'Shut up!' yelled Abu Samir, without any prompting from the two interrogators.

'You,' he said pointing to me, 'are a stupid, stubborn woman. Farzad has told us everything and he will be going home within a few days, whereas you will be going to prison for fifteen years.'

I gaped at him, speechless.

The tea-boy came in with a tray of coffee. Everyone except me was served. Lopsided spoke in Arabic and Abu Samir translated.

'One of you is lying and it isn't Farzad, so it must be you,' he said, glaring at me.

He turned to Farzad. 'Tell us again what happened.'

Farzad spoke quickly about the two trips to Hilla and the evenings we had spent together. He told them pretty much the same as I had. There was hardly any difference in our accounts at all. How then was I lying and Farzad telling the truth? My hopes began to soar. Could it be that we were actually going to get this sorted out? Could today be the day they realised they had made a mistake?

When Farzad had finished speaking, Abu Samir looked over at me. 'Do you agree with what Farzad says?' I was asked.

'Not entirely, but we differ only on minor points. I would agree with most of what he has said.'

'You told us that the guard at the gate of the explosion site waved over his shoulder and said "one kilometre", but Farzad tells us that the guard said "two kilometres". Who is lying?'

'Neither of us,' I replied. 'I thought the guard said "one kilometre", but since Farzad was in the passenger seat and closer to him than me, he is more likely to be correct. I concede the point.'

'Farzad tells us that you told him you always carry a camera with you whenever you go out, but you told us, when we asked, that you only occasionally carry a camera. Who is lying?'

So that was why the interrogators had kept harping on about the camera; it was something Farzad had said.

'Not me,' I jumped in quickly. 'I don't carry a camera with me every time I go out, only on sightseeing trips.'

Abu Samir turned to Farzad with a half-smile on his face. He was really on form today, determined to make me look like a liar and to nail me if he could.

'What, exactly, did she tell you?'

Farzad reached into the pocket of his brown-and-white-striped pyjama top and took out a pen and notepad. I stared at him enviously. He was really the good boy and I was the bad girl. He sat back in his comfy chair, had a sip of coffee and began reading aloud from his notepad.

'Dee pulled the car off the road and, for whatever reason, parked in front of the Presidential Palace. I was annoyed with her because I had my camera in the car and thought that if we were stopped and the camera found, its presence might be misconstrued. She replied, and I quote; "No problem, I carry a camera with me all the time." ' He closed the notepad.

I recalled the incident clearly. Farzad was worried because we were outside the Presidential Palace. After the protracted war with Iran, Iraqis were still sensitive about foreigners, particularly camera-carrying ones, outside the official residence of their leader. I had been trying to reassure him that I had never been hassled for simply being in possession of a camera and didn't think he would be either. However, Farzad's statement made my comment sound almost sinister.

'Do you deny this?' Abu Samir's eyes bored into mine.

I was going to have to play this very carefully; Abu Samir was having too good a time. He could smell blood – mine – and I was beginning to get frightened.

'Those may have been my words, but they weren't meant to be taken literally. It was a throwaway remark.'

'Did you or did you not use those words? Answer yes or no.'

'Yes, but I repeat, it's a misunderstanding.'

'Farzad told us you were smiling when you spoke to a man who had lost his leg in the war. Were you happy to see an Iraqi person injured? Were you pleased that an Iraqi was forced to walk with the aid of crutches?'

I was appalled at the suggestion and less frightened than angry that it should have been made.

'Of course not!' I protested loudly. 'I am a nurse, trained to help people in need, regardless of their nationality.'

'So, you are saying that you weren't smiling?'

'No, I'm saying that the man smiled at me and I smiled back at him. I was not amused by his war wounds. That is a preposterous idea.'

'When you were at the explosion site you came to a road sign which read "No Entry". Why did you drive past it?'

'I didn't see a "No Entry" sign. There was only one road sign, which read "Alexandria" in English.'

'What else was on the sign?'

'There was Arabic writing underneath. I can't read Arabic so I don't know what it said. I can only presume that it was the Arabic equivalent of the English written above, like a usual road sign in Iraq.'

The Gnome handed me a snapshot that Farzad had taken of the road sign on the second day we went to Hilla. Sure enough, the name Alexandria stood out clearly with the Arabic writing underneath – but what was that up in the corner? With a sinking heart, I could just make out the words 'No Entry'.

'This photograph was taken by Farzad. We have developed the film. Do you remember him taking this picture?'

I nodded dumbly.

'Sign here,' said Abu Samir. Again I was forced to sign the statement of my interrogation. This was the second time they had 'caught me out' in a lie – at least I knew that was how they would see it.

I had never felt so vulnerable. Abu Samir made a hand movement to Farzad who leaned forward, resting his hands on the coffee table.

'If we get these last points sorted out,' Farzad smiled across at me confidently. 'We can fly out of here together on Tuesday night. But first, Dee, you must tell them everything that happened. Look, all you have to say is that you became friendly with a British diplomat who persuaded you to go with me to the explosion site.'

'But that's not true, Farzad!' I exclaimed. 'You know perfectly well how I came to drive you to Hilla and there was nobody else involved.'

I was completely bewildered. Why was he saying these things? What did he mean by saying 'tell them everything' and what was all this business about a British diplomat? Could he have been subjected to torture? I scanned his face and hands for marks, but there were none.

'Just do it,' he urged, not smiling now.

'Look, Farzad, I've told them everything that happened, everything I know. There isn't any more.' I was angry now, angry with him for saying these things, angry that after hours of denying the interrogators' accusations that I was involved with spies and diplomats, he was now implying that I had been lying and had indeed been involved in some espionage plot.

'You can cut your own throat if you wish, but I'm staying with the truth!' I shouted across the table into his face.

Farzad's anger flared up immediately. He half-rose from his chair as if he intended to strike me. Abu Samir had also seen what was about to happen. He shot forward and yelled out, 'Put on your blindfolds!'

I was led away, shaking from yet another unexpected turn of events.

11 November 1989

The Ambassador
The Embassy of the Republic of Iraq

Your Excellency

I have written to you now on two previous occasions and as yet have received no reply. I write again to you to demand that my mother Mrs Daphne Parish is released from being detained incommunicado and given the consular access which she is lawfully entitled to under the Vienna Convention, which Iraq is party to.

While I am delighted that the British Embassy was able to see Mr Bazoft last week, I find it totally bewildering as to why my mother was denied such a visit.

I await to hear your thoughts on this matter and enclose a stamped addressed envelope for your reply.

Yours sincerely
Michelle de Vries

I didn't seem to be having much success with my attempts to petition the Iraqi authorities by letter. None of them prompted any response, so it was with great relief that I learned, later in November, that the Foreign Office had managed to arrange a meeting with an official from the Iraqi Embassy. Peter and I met up with Mark, a diplomat from the Foreign Office, at the top of Queen's Gate in London's Kensington. On the short walk to the Embassy Mark briefed us on what to expect.

'It is unusual for an Iraqi diplomat to see someone under such circumstances,' Mark explained. 'But Zuhair Ibrahim is a nice man, he is quite Westernised, and he felt that it would be good to talk to you about your mother's case. You will find him very pleasant and if he offers you any food or drink, you should accept out of politeness.'

Zuhair Ibrahim was a tall, slim man with grey hair.

'Mark, my friend, how are you?' He greeted us in a friendly manner. 'And you must be Michelle. Please, sit down. Would you like a sweet? Here, take two. You, Mark, do not need two, you are big enough already,' he joked. After several minutes of polite conversation, Zuhair Ibrahim straightened suddenly and looked towards me.

'Mark has told me that you are anxious to see your mother. I will see what I can do, but you must understand that she has committed a very grave offence against Iraq.'

I felt myself bristle. I hoped this meeting had not been arranged as an Iraqi propaganda exercise. I wanted to know what was happening. I wanted to see my mother, but I wasn't prepared to stand there and allow this man to condemn her for what I now knew had been nothing more than an innocent mistake.

'I sympathise with your country's view on the matter, but I can assure you that my mother never meant to cause any harm to Iraq.

She loves your country, she enjoyed her work there and would never have done anything to cause any harm to the Iraqi people,' I told Zuhair Ibrahim calmly.

'That may be true,' he responded, 'but you cannot dispute the fact that your mother and the journalist Bazoft visited an area which was strictly out of bounds to Westerners.'

'But they never penetrated the exclusion zone,' I interrupted. 'As I understand it, they just drove around the perimeter fence along a regularly-used highway.'

'Michelle, Michelle!' Zuhair Ibrahim put up his hand to stop me speaking. 'We, the Iraqi people, are a nation which has suffered terribly throughout the years. We are still in a cease-fire agreement with Iran, but the war is not yet over and we have a right to protect our country. The people at the Parc hospital hold a very privileged place in our society. Some say they are the happiest people in Iraq. We allow them freedom to travel freely through the desert, to visit our tourist attractions, to go to Basra in the south, Mosul in the north. They can travel where they want to, so why did your mother have to go to the area of Hilla, which is out of bounds to everyone?'

He shook his head in a resigned way, but I was ready for this one. My mother and Farzad had not been the only ones in Hilla that day.

'But as you know, Mr Ibrahim, many other journalists were also at that site investigating the report in the *Independent* newspaper that there had been an explosion there. Some of those journalists actually went into the prohibited area, climbed over the fence, and yet they were allowed to go free.'

'Farzad Bazoft was found with a test-tube of soil and some maps of the area. This is not the work of a journalist. We have the right to protect our country from the imperialists and the Zionist Satans who want to ruin us. We are a young country and our achievements in the last thirty years have been spectacular. Do you know that when Britain ruled over us in the early part of the century, there were no hospitals or schools for the Iraqi people? Today we have a one hundred per cent literacy rate, which is higher than you have here in England. We are constantly struggling against the Zionist Press over here, which has treated Iraq with disrespect and has blatantly lied about our human rights record and the intentions of our president. Do you now understand why we are so sensitive about such issues as this one involving your mother?'

I could see he was getting ruffled and the last thing I wanted to do was put anybody's back up. I needed all the friends I could get inside the Embassy. I smiled.

'All I ask is that both my mother and Farzad be given a fair trial and that they are both well treated.'

'Your mother is being well treated,' Zuhair Ibrahim assured me. 'In fact, she is being held in an apartment which is furnished even better than the room we are now in.'

I looked around the large room situated at the back of the Embassy, well furnished and decorated in various shades of red, and wondered about this man. He had said he would try to help me and I wanted to believe him, yet somehow I remained completely unconvinced.

A Very Special Message

It was a beautiful dream. Someone was running gentle fingers through my hair. I reached up to clasp the hand and caught hold of a huge cockroach instead.

'Aaaaargh! Aaaaargh!'

On hearing my screams a guard came running along the corridor, rubbing the sleep from his eyes and shouting at me in Arabic. I pointed to the cockroach scuttling across the floor. The guard smiled.

'*Mako muskular. Boukra* (No problem. Tomorrow),' he said, miming the action of spraying the cell and indicating that I should go back to sleep. But the thought of that monstrous bug anywhere near my person was enough to keep me awake for the rest of the night. I lay on my mattress, one hand clutching my shoe, one eye ever vigilant. Bug patrol was not an issue that I, with a lifelong horror of creepy-crawlies, could take lightly.

In the morning Hamid, the English-speaking guard who had recently returned to his work after an absence of several weeks, came to my cell with a can of insecticide spray.

'Why you scream in the night? The cockroaches are good because they eat all the smaller insects. If I kill the cock-roaches, your cell will fill with ants.'

'I don't care, Hamid, as long as there are no more cock-roaches. Please get rid of them for me.' This went against the grain, for I hate the idea of killing or maiming animals, but I had no option.

I sat outside in the corridor as Hamid sprayed my cell. My neighbour came to his hatch and looked out at me. He was tall and quite young, with black hair and olive skin. So this was the chap I sometimes heard pacing up and down, the one responsible for us spending almost twenty-four hours without water because he had allowed his washroom tap to deplete the entire supply. We stared at each other. As he turned the right side of his face to the hatch door I caught my breath. His face was heavily bruised, his right eye was closed and swollen and there was a considerable quantity of what appeared to be dried blood in his hair. He pointed to himself and put his hand to his neck, pushing his chin upwards. I later discovered that this indicated he was about to be hanged.

An old man came along the corridor carrying bundles of newspapers. My eyes fell on the English words *Baghdad Observer*.

'*Shweya, shweya, lo sat mat, ahmey, min fadlik* (Please excuse me)!' I pointed to the paper. '*Min fadlik*, please!' I repeated.

He handed it to me and walked on. I settled back on the floor, opened it up and read every word of the four-page newspaper. After about thirty minutes Hamid returned me to my cell and locked the door. The smell of insecticide was overwhelming, but far worse, cockroaches by the dozen were climbing out of the washroom drain, staggering drunkenly across the floor until they stopped, rolled on to their backs and, with a last desperate wave of their legs, died. The cell was full of gasping, dying cockroaches; it was horrifying. I kneeled on my mattress, a shoe in each hand ready to crush any survivor that might make it as far as my bed. There were none, but watching the seemingly agonising demise of so many bugs became too much for me to endure. Keeping a wary eye on the events taking place on the cell floor, I tiptoed over to the door, terrified one of the creatures would gather together its last reserves of energy and make a mad dash for me.

'Hamid!' I screamed through the hatch. He clearly thought I was off my head, but returned anyway and swept the remaining bodies down the drain.

'Now,' he warned me as his parting shot, 'you will have ants.'

How right he was. I awoke the next morning with a line of ants moving up my face, over my nose and into my hair. There was a second battalion marching towards me across the floor. I shook and beat the ants out of my hair and off my body and attacked the advancing troops with my trusty shoe, wondering all the while, dear God, when will this nightmare end?

I don't know exactly when my mind turned to thoughts of escape, but after more than two and a half months in solitary confinement, I was convinced that if I was going to get out of prison, I would have to do it myself. I had heard nothing from the hospital, the British Embassy or any member of my family. For all I knew they might be thinking I was dead. I hadn't formulated any specific escape plan, but I was working with possibilities. For some weeks I had been digging out the damp plaster around my washroom tap. It was a painstaking job: my only tools were my fingers and although the plaster was fairly soft, it was still painful to gouge out for more than a few minutes at a time. I went back to the washroom time and time again over the course of a day, to poke and scrape around the tap. I felt certain it was an outside wall, and knowing what the general standard of plumbing in the interrogation block was like, I reckoned if I could just get through the plaster, I might have a window on the outside world.

One afternoon in late November I was scraping away in a rather desultory fashion, keeping an eye out for anyone appearing at the hatch, when I felt the plaster give beneath my fingers. As quietly as I could I began yanking the tap forwards and pushing it back. The plaster cracked but didn't, as I hoped it might, fall out. Back to probing and scraping, but now, with mounting excitement about what lay on the other side, I worked with a will. It was probably twenty minutes before the first decent-sized lump of plaster, about the size of a thumbnail, fell to the ground. It had not been easy, but I knew immediately it had been worth it. A shaft of light hit the greasy washroom floor. Daylight.

I knelt down and looked through the peephole to the outside world I had created. A corner of the car park sprang into view, with a gate through which lay freedom. Lovely green trees stood beyond the gate and small white clouds drifted across a dazzling blue sky. The view was as wonderful to me as any work of art I had ever seen, after being locked up without sight of so much as a blade of grass for all these weeks, but I didn't spend long looking at it; I had seen what I needed to see. I loosely packed the stone and plaster back into the hole and returned to my mattress.

I picked up the *Baghdad Observer* and turned to the weather forecast. A light south-westerly wind, it said. Wonderful. I had seen through my peephole which way the clouds were moving, so now I knew which way we were facing and our approximate position in relation to the River Tigris. I have always had a good sense of direction. When I walk around an unknown town or city I make mental notes of whether I am heading east or west, on which side I pass the town hall, or a particular cinema, or theatre. I have done it for years and it's an automatic thing with me now. So, now I had a pretty good idea of where I was geographically, I could work out which direction to head for should the opportunity to cut and run ever arise.

Several days had passed since the meeting with Farzad, when he had looked as if he was about to punch me. Whatever the interrogators had hoped to achieve by allowing us to meet they had clearly failed. Even so, I felt fairly sure that they would not leave it there, and I was proved right. A key turned in the lock. Ahmed held out a blindfold. We went to the interrogation centre where Farzad was sitting in a comfortable chair, smoking a cigarette and drinking a glass of coffee. A small wooden straight-backed chair had been placed opposite him and this is where it was indicated I should sit. As I sat down, the telephone rang and as the Gnome settled back in his chair, obviously preparing for a long chat, I realised that neither Lopsided nor Abu Samir had yet appeared. It was too good an opportunity to miss.

'Farzad,' I hissed, 'why did you make the video?'

Speaking out of the side of his mouth to avoid being seen by the Gnome, he replied, 'I had to, because of the electric shocks.'

Whether Farzad had actually received electric shocks, or whether he had just been threatened with this horrible form of torture, I was never to find out, because at that moment Abu Samir came into the room. A guard brought fresh coffee for Abu Samir and Farzad, but not for me. Farzad leaned back in his armchair looking for all the world as if he were in his own sitting-room at home. The Gnome was still on the telephone.

'The *Observer* newspaper rang up to ask after you, Farzad,' said Abu Samir, 'but,' he said, looking at me with an expression approaching regret, 'no one has enquired about you.'

Stunned by what he had said, I was only vaguely aware of the Gnome finishing his telephone call, picking up a file from the desk and hurrying from the room, calling over his shoulder to Abu Samir in Arabic as he left. The interview never took place.

I was taken back to my cell, where I lay on the mattress staring up at the ceiling. No one had telephoned to ask about me! Surely that couldn't be true. Michelle would be going out of her mind with worry, as would Martina, my brother Alan, my sisters and friends. But perhaps they weren't even aware that I had been arrested. Perhaps they were only just beginning to wonder why I hadn't written lately, possibly putting it down to the vagaries of the postal system. What about the hospital? Maybe Dr Raad and the Director of Nursing had decided to hush the whole thing up. And what was going on with Farzad? He had gone on record saying he was a spy and now he was being treated like a hero.

The interrogators' treatment of Farzad was something I had not been able to make sense of since our first meeting. Even as he had been urging me to confess to things I had not done, I had the feeling he was not doing so of his own free will. Although he had made me very angry then, I had since had time to reflect. Just now he had talked of electric shocks. I shuddered to think.

I felt totally abandoned, and, in my isolation, half-believed that no one knew or cared what had happened to me. Tears flowed on to the pillow. I knew, even as I felt them trickle down my face, that the last thing I could afford at this stage was self-pity. 'Get up and do something, woman!' I told myself sternly. I knew that if I could just get the impression that I was alone and totally forgotten out of my head, I would be all right. I began to do some aerobic exercises and almost immediately felt a little better. Twenty minutes later I was back in control. Right, what next? I was bored with Scrabble: the most fascinating game loses its attraction after being played a dozen times a day. I sat down on my mattress again and began to fashion a paper dart out of a column of the *Baghdad Observer*. I aimed at the squashed fly on the cell wall. Hey, wait a minute, why not make a dartboard?

I went to the washroom, where I had hidden the small stump of a lead pencil I had fairly recently managed to steal from the interrogation room. I began to sketch the outline of a dartboard on the wall above the head of my mattress, where the guards couldn't see. It was painfully-slow work, as the rough stone wall of my cell quickly blunted the pencil and I had to stop frequently to resharpen it on the stone step of the washroom. Now where to put the numbers? I remembered that 20 went up at the top, with 1 next to it, number 3 was down at the bottom, flanked by 17 and 19. The number 11 went at the nine o'clock position, with a 12 and 5 leading up to the 20, but where did the other numbers go? Whoever designed the dartboard must have had a logical reason for placing the numbers in certain positions. I sat down on the mattress to work it out. There must be a pattern somewhere. I put 20 opposite 3 and 11 opposite 10 and then went through every computation I could think of, but there seemed to be no answer to the puzzle. I fitted the numbers around the board as best I could before making two columns next to the dart-board, one headed 'thee', the other 'me'. My imaginary partner for this game was male, a shadowy figure who won the first match we ever played together.

Someone was shouting in the corridor; that probably meant that Bad News had come on duty. Better stop the dart game and keep my head down. I heard him screaming at my next-door neighbour to return his newspaper and I quickly pulled the partially-torn middle section out of the *Baghdad Observer* so that I could hand him the front and back pages, which always carried pictures of Saddam Hussein. I wondered what the guards did with all these pictures. It was an offence to deface a picture of the President or even to throw a newspaper containing one in the waste-paper bin. The cupboards and drawers of Iraqis must be stuffed full of pictures of Saddam, I thought. Bad News glowered through the hatch. I handed over what remained of the paper with a smile and settled down on my mattress for an early night.

One morning in early December, Hamid woke me at 6 a.m.

'First you wash yourself, then I take you downstairs to speak with the Chief,' he instructed.

The Chief Interrogator sat behind a highly-polished desk in a larger, more luxuriously furnished room than the one along the corridor where I usually saw the two beauties, Lopsided and the Gnome. Although I had managed to lose them for this meeting, the hated interpreter, Abu Samir, was present, wearing his usual sardonic smile. However, I quickly noticed that there was something very different about him today in the presence of the big boss. Where was the confident bully who frequently didn't bother to wait for guidance from the two beauties, but made his own bitingly-sarcastic remarks off the cuff? He had, it seemed, been replaced by a fawning, crawling specimen, constantly begging the Chief's pardon, serving him coffee, waiting for him to complete a sentence before beginning to translate it. I was astonished at the transformation.

'We are considering,' he translated for the Chief, 'but only considering, allowing you to meet the people from your

Embassy. However, you must understand that you are not to say anything.'

So they did know where I was. Thank God! Deep down I had felt that they must, but there was always the nagging doubt that people on the outside might think I had simply disappeared. This was all the confirmation I needed.

'Not say anything!' I was astounded. 'You must be mad! Of course I shall say something. I need food, clean clothes, books, messages . . .'

'These things you can speak about,' Abu Samir interrupted. 'Other things, not. We think you understand what we mean.'

The penny dropped. 'I see,' I said carefully. 'You are suggesting, are you not, that I should say nothing about being kicked and having my hair pulled. Say nothing about being kept blindfold and threatened with a knife, nor of being told that I would have my clothes taken away and be made to stand up all night. Should I keep quiet about the threats made in your presence, Abu Samir, that I would be beaten and smashed against the wall?'

The Chief and Abu Samir spoke quietly together in Arabic. Both wore uncomfortable expressions.

I felt a heady kind of power. After three months of deprivation, isolation, fear and hunger, suddenly I held the cards. Foolishly, I let it go straight to my head.

'Let us not deprive the British Press of such interesting little titbits! To know, amongst other things, that I am being held in a cell infested with ants and cockroaches would make for a good read, would it not?' I stopped triumphantly. Abu Samir glared at me with ill-disguised hatred.

'You will not say these things!'

'Oh, and how do you propose stopping me?' I asked with a wry smile.

'We shall not allow the visit . . .'

I was power-crazed by this point. Every time I opened my mouth it was as if my brain fell out, but even though I knew I was sailing desperately close to the wind I couldn't stop.

'Ah, but you will. You see, I happen to know there is a rumour going around that I am already dead, tortured, perhaps by the interrogators. You have to show me to British Embassy staff to prove I'm alive.'

Abu Samir conferred with the Chief, consternation all over their faces. Oh, sweet revenge!

'Where you hear this thing?' Abu Samir was so rattled he lapsed into pidgin English. It did my heart good to hear it. I felt on top of the world, but I realised that I couldn't afford to be too foolhardy. I desperately needed the visit. My family must be frantic, and besides, I must not get the nice inter-preter, the one with the scarred nose, into trouble. Yesterday he had told me at a 'welfare' visit that the time had come for me to be shown to the Embassy staff to prove that I was alive. Even though I liked him, I hadn't let my hopes run away with me. Iraqi people hate to be bearers of bad news. It sounds odd to Western ears, but time and time again at the hospital I had seen Iraqi staff go out of their way to mislead distraught relatives of patients who were clearly terminally ill by insist-ing there was hope. It is not unkindly meant, quite the reverse, but I had learned long ago that it was not wise to believe all I was told. However, it now seemed that the interpreter might have been telling the truth. I decided to change tack.

'One does not need to be of superior intelligence to work these things out,' I told him. 'However,' I went on, 'I do not intend to waste my visit talking about this crazy place.'

Abu Samir had noticed this subtle backing down. Now he was in control again and it showed. A look of contempt crossed his face.

'You will not refer to this building as a crazy place. You will have respect for the Iraqi law and remember, we have the power to stop the visit at any time during the hour allowed. Now get out, put on your blindfold and wait outside with your face against the wall.'

Like a naughty schoolgirl I stood outside the door of the interrogation room, but I felt like singing. During the months I had been locked up here I had experienced huge mood swings. Some days I would be in desperation wondering why no one had contacted me. In this frame of mind it was all too easy to convince myself that nobody knew where I was, nobody cared and that considering the paltry amount it must cost to feed me, the Iraqi Government could keep me in here for ever, if they chose to do so. On other days I would be filled with hope, seeing the length of time I had already spent here as so many days and months nearer to when I would be allowed to go home. A message, a letter, a visit could only be around the corner, I would convince myself. As I reflected on this I heard a man's voice behind me.

'Hello, Dee.'

Turning around and tilting my head back, I looked out from under my blindfold and saw Abdullah, the guard from the hospital who had yelled at me the last time I had seen and recognised him. Abdullah stood with his hands behind his back, dressed not in his customary green military uniform but in a grey suit, white shirt and multicoloured tie.

'I shall be going with you to the Ministry of Foreign Affairs,' he told me.

'Are we going now?' I asked incredulously. Could this be true: after almost three lonely months I learn I'm to get a visit and actually get that visit all in the same day? I didn't know whether to feel elated or cheated. It took a micro-second to settle on the former.

'Yes, we are leaving now,' he replied.

I was genuinely delighted he was there. 'Thank goodness you're coming,' I said, with a sigh of relief. 'I thought I was going to have to spend the morning with that snake Abu Samir breathing down my neck and ruining my day.'

Abdullah threw back his head and laughed. 'I'm sorry to tell you, Dee, but he's coming along as well.'

Sitting in the back of the car between two guards and accompanied by Abdullah and Abu Samir I attempted to collect my thoughts, but the very idea of at last being able to talk to someone from England was overwhelming. The car left the covered car park, passed through the gate I could see from my washroom peephole, and joined the stream of traffic heading towards the Arbah Bridge.

Initially, my eyes felt extremely painful as they attempted to adjust to the bright morning sunlight streaming through the car windows, but as I became accustomed to the intensity of brightness, the pain subsided and I realised where we were. We passed the Melia Hotel where Farzad and I had first had dinner together, also the scene of so many laughter-filled evenings in the bar with other expatriate friends. As we entered the gates of the Foreign Ministry I glanced at the wrist-watch worn by the guard on the right. Abdullah had told me the meeting was scheduled for eleven o'clock, but it was only ten minutes past nine. What on earth were we going to do for almost two hours? In fact the time passed quickly enough as one foreign face after another warned me about what not to say at the meeting. I was not to talk about my cell or the building where I was being held, the interrogators (they called them officers), the guards or the food. I was not to mention Farzad or any meetings with him. On and on and on the instructions went.

We were sitting in a comfortable room, furnished with a sofa, two armchairs and a coffee table. Five more upright chairs were brought in to seat Abdullah, two staff members from the Ministry, and a guard. Today, I was in an armchair, but too tense to appreciate it.

I could hear voices, speaking English, approaching down the corridor. My mouth went dry and my heart felt as if it were somewhere in the region of my tonsils. We all stood up as Robin Kealy, First Secretary of the British Embassy, and Pauline Waugh, the Consul, entered the room. I had met both of them before briefly at various functions and I'd been to Robin's house with Farzad, but it was a big gathering and there was no reason why he should have remembered me. There were handshakes and introductions all round before we sat down. Robin and Pauline sat side by side on the sofa, facing me across the coffee table, while Abu Samir made his presence felt in an armchair placed right next to mine.

It was all very British. Robin leaned forward, concern etched across his features.

'We have repeatedly tried to gain access to you and at last we have succeeded. How are you, Dee?'

'Well, I'm fine,' I said, lying through my teeth, but afraid to say anything else in case, as Abu Samir had warned, the meeting would be terminated. Was this, I wondered, how Farzad had felt when he was put in front of a camera and forced to make his video?

'We've got lots of messages for you,' Robin said with a smile and proceeded to read out a list of friends and colleagues from the hospital, and family and friends in England.

'And, of course,' he went on, 'a very special message from your daughter Michelle.'

That was the last straw for me. I was unable to contain my feelings a moment longer and I burst into tears, great long, racking sobs I had been trying to hold back for weeks. Nothing the interrogators had done or would do could possibly have made me feel worse than I did at that moment. Throwing all caution to the wind I sobbed out the sorry state of my health, the diarrhoea, vomiting, headaches, toothache, weight loss, infections, cramp and numbness of fingers and toes, conditions I had been trying to play down even to myself because I was frightened to face what they meant – that I probably wouldn't be able to tolerate the conditions in which I was living for much longer without running the risk of a very serious breakdown in health.

'Most of all, though,' I sniffled through the tears, 'I need something to take my mind off all these problems. I have nothing to do, I've spent weeks, months doing nothing!'

'We've been able to do something about that,' said Robin. 'We've brought you a box of books, collected by your friends at the hospital, and the Ambassador's wife has sent along a copy of The Shell Seekers, which she personally recommends. We've also brought food, Complan, powdered milk, coffee, cheese, biscuits, tinned foods and chocolate.'

Now I sobbed harder than ever. 'Oh, thank you, thank you, that's wonderful.' Pauline, who had been taking notes, asked Abu Samir if dental treatment could be arranged for my toothache.

'Certainly,' he said smoothly. 'She only has to ask and all these things will be taken care of, but for now,' he glanced at his watch, 'the meeting must end.'

We all stood up. We'd been together an hour, but it didn't seem like it. Pauline gave me a big hug, Robin shook hands.

'We shall press for another meeting in January. Oh yes,' and he smiled, 'Merry Christmas!'

How could he say such a thing to someone who was going to spend Christmas in a cell alone? I broke into a fresh paroxysm of weeping, as Pauline and Robin were escorted away.

'Shut up!' ordered Abu Samir. 'And stop the crocodile tears. Farzad also tried that at his meeting. Big babies,' he sneered.

'Hamid,' I asked him for the umpteenth time, 'where is my box of food?' It was ten days since the visit of Robin and Pauline, when I had watched my box of goodies loaded into the boot of the car and brought back with us into the interrogation centre. Just thinking about powdered milk and chocolate made me salivate like one of Pavlov's dogs.

'Nobody knows,' said Hamid. 'Maybe it was left in the car.'

'And maybe it wasn't,' I replied angrily. For ten long days I had waited for that box, or even a packet of biscuits from it, to appear at my cell door. I had fantasised about the taste of every conceivable foodstuff since Robin had mentioned 'tinned foods'; in my mind I had pictured a hundred of my favourite books. Damn it, even in my dreams I no longer wandered down English country lanes; instead I lay on my mattress, eating a Terry's Chocolate Orange whilst reading a totally absorbing, racy novel full of carefree beautiful people and set in the Mediterranean.

'Maybe,' I yelled at poor Hamid, probably my best friend in here and certainly not the person deserving of my wrath, 'maybe at this very moment it is sitting on shelves at the homes of the interrogators.'

'I will try and find out,' said Hamid in a soothing voice. He didn't come back.

'Thieves!' I yelled through the hatch door a few hours later in a cocktail of hunger, rage, anticipation and frustration. 'The interrogators are Ali Baba's forty thieves. Thieves, thieves, thieves!'

Bad News came stomping down the corridor looking like thunder. Hamid must have gone off duty. He opened my cell and manhandled me along the corridor and into the lift. Abdullah sat behind the desk of the interrogation room.

'Whatever is the matter, Dee?'

'Someone has stolen my food and my books,' I sobbed. He had been there, he knew exactly what I was talking about.

Abdullah reached under the desk and lifted up a small cardboard box. 'Here is your food. You must understand that everything has to be checked. Those are the regulations.'

So, he'd had them there all along; he'd been keeping them from me.

'Not for ten days! For goodness sake, we are talking about a few tins and a handful of books. You knew . . . Oh, never mind, please give me some chocolate.'

'You can take the box and two books.'

He reached into a second box, and pulled out two books at random and handed them to me.

I looked down at the covers. One of the books was a Tom Stoppard play, the other Erich Segal's *The Class*. The tension was broken and I couldn't stop laughing. I had read *The Class* a few years previously and knew it leaned heavily towards the Jewish race and the Zionist cause in particular. After all these months of being accused of being a Jew and a spy for Israel I was being given what many people would classify as a Zionist tract. I felt my body beginning to shake with laughter.

'Why are you laughing?' asked Abdullah.

'No reason, Abdullah. I'm just feeling a little high. May I go back to my cell?' I was impatient, desperate to get my hands on the food.

I put myself on a strict ration. One packet of Complan, one biscuit and one square of chocolate a day. Somehow it didn't really work. I would find myself creeping down the mattress, reaching into the box like a thief in the night to extract yet another piece of the delicious orange-flavoured chocolate. Because there was no way of heating water, I mixed coffee and powdered milk with cold water from the tap, using a teaspoon I had taken from the interrogation room. Actually, I had got the idea from Farzad. Since seeing him dextrously slip a packet of cigarettes and a box of matches inside his notebook during a joint interrogation and later put them in his pocket, I had used every interrogation session since as an opportunity to take something.

Does being a prisoner make thieves of us all? I wondered. I squared my conscience by telling myself that I hadn't actually taken it out of the building, just moved it a couple of flights upstairs.

I went into the washroom, reached up to the ledge and retrieved my pencil stub and the empty cigarette packet (acquired in the same way) to write my diary. The pencil was blunt again, so I sharpened it on the edge of the stone step leading up to the washroom, straightened out the cigarette packet and reread my entries for the last two weeks.

Tuesday 5 December: Taken to meet Robin and Pauline from the British Embassy.
Wednesday 6 December: Lost in thought.
Thursday 7 December: Again lost in thought, but took a little exercise with the ball.

Those 'lost thoughts' were spent rehashing every word that passed across the coffee table at the Ministry of Foreign Affairs. I had spent hours puzzling over Robin's last words. 'Merry Christmas,' he had said. I was sure it hadn't been a gaffe: he was too experienced a diplomat for that. It couldn't mean that I was going to be released or it wouldn't have been necessary for him to press for a January meeting. He had been trying to tell me something, I was sure, but what? I went over the whole conversation again and again, sentence by sentence. If only I hadn't been so emotional, there might not be so many gaps in my memory. And then the words came back to me. 'Michelle hopes to be able to visit.' That was it, it must be?

Michelle was coming out. Yes, that was it, I was sure. I sat up in the corner of my cell shielding the pen and paper from prying eyes that might look through the cell-door hatch, and continued bringing my diary up to date.

Sunday 17 December: Taken downstairs and given box of groceries. More books promised the day after tomorrow. Immediately ate chocolate, a cream cheese and biscuit. Made coffee with powdered milk. I wonder if Michelle is coming soon. Last night I couldn't get her out of my thoughts. In view of what Robin said, i.e. 'Merry Christmas', I'm wondering. It seems even more likely, but don't count your chickens before they're hatched. One week today is Christmas Eve.

'Dear God, please make Saddam Hussein realise that my mother is innocent, that she loves Iraq and the Iraqi people and would never do anything to harm the country.' I was praying – out loud – not for the ears of God but rather, I hoped, giving a clear message to the Iraqi secret police. I was sure they were bugging my room.

Peter and I were staying at the Al Rashid Hotel. It was our first night in the Middle East. Our only previous knowledge of the country was scant, gleaned from my mother's letters and television coverage during the Iran-Iraq War. Our first sight of the country had been quite a revelation. 'My God, there are lights down there,' I said to Peter, looking out of the aircraft window as the pilot announced our descent into Baghdad. Below us lay not the small desert town I had imagined, but a vast sprawling city, illuminated by what seemed like millions of orange lights.

We were met at the airport by Pauline Waugh, the British Consul, and a representative from Parc. We drove together to the Al Rashid Hotel, made famous during the Gulf War when it was the base for most of the foreign journalists covering the action from Baghdad. I was impressed by the five-lane highways and the magnificent Fourteenth of July Bridge, later destroyed in the war. The skyline was dominated by towering office blocks and enormous monuments, brightly lit in red, green, white and black, the colours of the Iraqi flag.

Several hours later, unable to sleep, I stood on my balcony listening to the endless tooting of car horns in the street below. Dawn was breaking. I gazed across the River Tigris, beyond the white, flat-roofed, war-damaged buildings where groups of Iraqi soldiers manned anti-aircraft missiles pointing towards the sky. Last night the city had seemed romantic, but in the glimmering light of day it appeared shabby and sinister. I wondered where, among the sprawling mass of concrete below, they were holding my mother. I wondered if she even knew we were here.

A British diplomat I had spoken to yesterday in London had warned me not to be optimistic. 'Remember, the Iraqis have not officially promised anything. Don't arrive in Baghdad convinced that you will see your mother. The officials are quite likely to turn round at the last minute and deny you access,' he had stressed. I appreciated his candour, but it was impossible not to feel some optimism.

After spending two weeks holiday from her annual leave in England, my mother had returned to Baghdad on 23 August. We are close and get on well together. Unusually, we had had a blazing row shortly before her departure. It blew up over a minor issue and had got completely out of hand, possibly because I was upset she was going back to Baghdad. I knew how much she loved her job and her life in Iraq and I would never really have wanted her to give that up. Although I had a full life of my own, she was still my mother and I sometimes missed having her around. When she was away we spoke on the telephone every couple of weeks and exchanged letters, but it wasn't the same as having her in London. A thousand times I had recalled what were almost my last words to her: 'Well go back to bloody Iraq then, and stay there!'

That was four months ago, and now I was standing on a hotel balcony watching dawn rise above this city she had so enjoyed living in. When I first learned she had been arrested I was desperately angry with her. I felt sure she must have been out on some madcap trip through the desert. She had spoken frequently about desert trips she had made with friends. I felt sure she had unknowingly driven into a restricted area and the misunderstanding would soon be cleared up.

When I discovered the truth of what had happened, my anger was transferred to the Iraqi authorities. How could they believe my mother, a fun-loving but totally dedicated and professional nurse, would be involved in espionage? I didn't know Farzad, but I did know my mother. I wasn't surprised that she hadn't been seen admitting anything on video. My mother can be a determined, even stubborn woman – she is also one of the most honest people I have ever known. She would not admit to something she had not done. I had never doubted that she would be able to cope with whatever the Iraqi authorities threw at her. I wasn't sure I had her strength, and wondered what the coming day would bring.

I reviewed the itinerary Pauline had given me the previous night.

8.30 a.m. – Embassy car to collect Peter and Michelle

9.00 a.m. – Briefing at the British Embassy

11.00 a.m. – Robin Kealy, Pauline Waugh, Michelle and Peter
to visit Daphne Parish

What would happen after eleven o'clock was anyone's guess, but for the moment we had forty-five minutes before the Embassy car arrived. Breakfast seemed to be a good way of filling the time.

Walking into the dining-room, Peter and I commented on how very hungry we both felt, probably because in all the excitement neither of us had had a meal the previous day. Our mouths watered at the sight of the lavish display awaiting us. A long table, covered in a white cloth and attractively decorated with flowers and gold-coloured streamers, was set out with a selection of delicious-looking dishes. There was no menu, so it was impossible to tell how much the breakfast buffet cost per head, but we were too hungry to worry about the price and, given that we only had just over half an hour to spare, we decided to go ahead. A waiter was bound to show up sooner or later. Not all the food was familiar to us, but we decided to start with eggs and muffins, helping ourselves to generous amounts.

I noticed that several of the other diners appeared to be staring over at us and, obviously amused, then began chatting animatedly among themselves. None of them appeared to be eating, they just looked and giggled. It must have been the way I was dressed. Was my skirt too short for an Islamic country? I decided to change before we left for the Embassy: the last thing I wanted to do was get anybody's back up. Then I looked up and noticed a young couple entering the dining-room. They were obviously famous because their entrance was met with a sudden burst of loud conversation and some applause. I looked again but didn't recognise them – perhaps they were Iraqi singers or film stars. The man was dressed in a smart black suit and the woman was heavily made-up and wore a long, elegant dress.

A waiter came hurrying towards our table, looking very perplexed.

'Are you guests of the family?' he enquired.

'Sorry?' I asked. What was the man talking about? 'Which family?'

'I think you misunderstand,' he replied, by now very flustered. 'This is not the hotel dining-room. This is one of the rooms we have for special receptions. The couple who just came in are getting married today. You are eating their wedding breakfast.'

We made a hurried departure, smiling apologetically to the wedding guests around the room, and were escorted to the hotel coffee shop. In contrast this room was furnished with plastic chairs and tables and the buffet bar was offering only a small selection of fairly unappetising food. We ordered a pot of coffee, more to kill time than anything else, and were presented with a bill for twenty-three pounds. Unless we could gatecrash a few more weddings Iraq, we realised, was going to be very expensive indeed.

Waiting for Pauline's arrival in the hotel lobby, I was surprised to see a sign which read: 'Welcome to the Al Rashid Hotel. Have a very Merry Christmas.' The sign was perched next to a tall plastic fir tree in the corner of the reception area. What was a Christmas tree doing in a Muslim country? I wondered. I later learned that, at that time, Iraq was considered one of the more moderate Gulf countries. Neighbouring Iran and Saudi Arabia operate a strict Islamic regime, but Iraq, although also an Islamic state, is far less conservative. The more free and easy Gulf states, such as Bahrain and the United Arab Emirates, are where expatriates employed in the Gulf still love to fly off to for weekends. Both are very Westernised. Iraq seemed to me to be very much a Middle Eastern country but with Western influences, probably because until 1918 it was governed, like many of the countries in the region, by the British. There are no pubs as such, but drinks are served in the hotels and although most of the women I saw on the streets of Baghdad were covered from head to toe in the black Islamic *chador*, the wearing of it is not compulsory.

Pauline arrived with the news that I would be able to see my mother at 11.30. As we walked together through the lobby I felt uneasy. There were quite a number of Iraqi soldiers posted in and around the Al Rashid Hotel and dozens of pairs of dark eyes seemed to leer at me from beneath military caps. With all the hatred I could muster I defiantly stared back at the enemy, for that is how I undoubtedly regarded them. They were members of the Iraqi armed forces, loyal to Saddam Hussein and therefore against me. Seeing my glare some of them smiled sweetly, others just giggled.

'You can't wear that in Iraq!' These were my mother's first words to me as we entered the room at the Ministry of Foreign Affairs. I was taken aback, stunned for a moment, then I began to weep hysterically. I hadn't expected to see her so soon and without any of the ceremony the Iraqis seemed to insist on for every minor movement. There had been no security check, no briefing. We had simply entered the Ministry building, been shown into a room and there she was, my mother. I hadn't had time to prepare myself for how she would look and I was deeply shocked.

As I hugged her for the first time in four months I realised how much weight she had lost. She had never been big, but hugging her now, she was like a child in my arms. Her face was ashen, her beautiful blonde hair thin, dry and wiry, her teeth discoloured and her eyes red and glazed. I'm ashamed to admit that I couldn't look her in the eye. I was too frightened by what I saw there and much too frightened that she would see my horror. This was my mother, for God's sake! How could I not want to look at her? Instead, I scanned the faces of the enemy. There were seven of them in the room, seated in chairs around a coffee table. They appeared hostile to my mother and to the rest of us. I wanted to hug her, to reassure her. More than anything in the world I wanted to get her out of that place. But I couldn't say anything of what I was feeling. I knew that this meeting could be brought to a close in an instant if I did the wrong thing. It was difficult to know what to talk about, what was safe ground. A question about the food prompted a weaselly-looking man to stop playing with his string of worry beads and snap: 'This is not a five-star hotel.'

'What do you do all day?'

My mother threw up her hands in frustration. 'Nothing! I sit in my cell. I look at the walls . . .'

'You can watch television in my office every night,' the weaselly man interrupted again. 'You only have to ask and we will make things easier for you.'

My mother raised her eyebrows but said nothing.

'What is the cell like?' I asked, desperate now to get some sort of conversation going before our time together ran out.

'She is not allowed to discuss that,' said a grey-haired man in an ill-fitting suit, with a glare in my direction.

Only one of the men in the room appeared in any way sympathetic. Of course, I couldn't discuss it with my mother, but I felt that he, at least, was quite human, and he was handsome, too. I hoped he was one of the people taking care of her in the interrogation centre. He did not scowl, nor did he wear that supercilious grin I had by now seen a number of times on the faces of Iraqi officials. On later visits this man, Abu Samir, proved himself to be quite a charmer, greeting me with kisses and enquiries about my wedding plans. He was the only Iraqi official I ever met that I felt I could put my trust in. In the hope that it would improve things for my mother, but also because I genuinely liked him, I would joke with him, bring him books and magazines from England to help him improve his English, and small presents for his young son. Abu Samir, how you betrayed me! It was not until months later I was to discover that you were my mother's chief tormentor.

In Abu Samir, I had misread the Iraqi perspective, something I was frequently to do in the future. He pulled the wool over my eyes, as did Iraq. As I got to know the country for its charm, its shabbiness, its history and its humble, kindly people, as I began to see beauty in its ornate mosques and its winding back streets, where toothless men sold copper and silks, I had to keep reminding myself that this was the country that was holding my mother and several thousand other innocent victims prisoner. That beneath its sophisticated, liberal exterior bubbled the sinister and oppressive machinations of Saddam Hussein's evil regime. A regime that held young children in prisons as pawns if their parents opposed the Government; a regime that massacred hundreds of Kurds, men, women and children, because their very existence offended Saddam Hussein; a regime that Westerners, in general, were ignorant of and foreign governments chose to ignore – until Saddam's troops moved into Kuwait in the summer of 1990, and by then it was too late.

Jingle Bells

Silent night, Holy night
All is calm, all is bright . . .

It was Christmas Day. I had saved my favourite carol for this special morning. I've always loved music, and though I'm the first to admit I don't have a great voice, it does carry; the sound echoed around the cell, flowed through the hatch and along the corridor. Abdul Rahmed heard it and smiled without understanding the words, as he handed out sweet black tea from his trolley.

'Happy Christmas, Abdul Rahmed!'

He returned my smile with a toothy grin and trundled off along the corridor with his trolley. I put the cup on the floor and reached for the tiny Harrod's Christmas cake Michelle had brought me. It was exquisite, but so small: I decided to have half now and the other half at tea-time, British tea-time that is, when all the people I loved and cared about would be cutting their cakes at home.

As I savoured the dark, rich cake, my thoughts drifted back to a recent Christmas morning in England, when I had shared a considerably larger chunk of cake and a glass of chilled champagne with Michelle. Our London flat, less sparsely furnished now thanks to the tax-free salary I had been earning in the Middle East but still lacking curtains in some of the rooms, was bright and festive. I recalled the huge Christmas tree we had bought and decorated with traditional coloured lights. Returning home from work at a busy London hospital one crisp, dark, late December evening, I had spotted them shining brightly in our flat window and marvelled as I walked up the road at how cheerful and welcoming they looked.

After my Christmas morning celebration with Michelle, I had spent the day sailing down the Thames on a friend's boat. We collected the boat from its moorings near the Isle of Dogs in London's East End and sailed right up the river. It was a freezing day and we were both wrapped up until we resembled Michelin men in yellow oilskins, but we had great fun. Dusk had fallen by about four o'clock and all the bridges were lit up; even the cranes had been specially decorated with lights and Christmas messages. It all seemed a very long time ago, light years away from this solitary Iraqi cell. What strange things fate, or whatever it is, throws at us.

Religion has never played a large part in my life. As a child I went to church and Sunday school, in fact I even remember – like so many people of my age – having a yen towards the evangelical school in the 1950s. I believe in God and I sometimes pray, but I am not, and haven't been for many years, a church-goer: weddings and funerals are about my limit. Even so, Christmas has always been a special time for me, a time for family and friends, and my thoughts that day were constantly with those at home.

My parents had always made Christmas a special time and I had tried to do the same for Michelle and, later, my step-daughter Martina. More than twenty years earlier, when Michelle was very small and I was very broke, we spent our first Christmas alone. The high-living days of the Bahamas now far behind us, I had filled her stocking with colourful, twopenny-halfpenny things from Woolworths. With childhood memories in my mind, much more for me than for her I now realise, I had gone out on Christmas Eve and bought a doll for £2.50. To me the doll, with her curly blonde hair, opening and closing eyes, long lashes and starched blue-and-white-striped dress, was the epitome of every toddler's Christmas dream. I spent more on that single present than I had on our Christmas dinner, and I was full of anticipation and self-congratulation as I arranged the doll, arms out-stretched, in the top of her stocking. On Christmas morning I could hardly wait for Michelle to wake and see the goodies Father Christmas had brought.

When she did finally toddle down to the bottom of her bed the first thing she did was pull my/her doll out of the stocking by the hair, toss it aside and swiftly get down to the far more interesting business of wax crayons, tangerines and colouring books. She spent the entire Christmas trying to lose that doll: she hated it. Eventually I gave it away. My daughter has always had a very independent spirit, something I would later thank God for.

This year, of course, there had been none of the traditional countdown to Christmas. The number of shopping days couldn't have been less relevant: since September, I'd had no access to shops to buy cards or gifts. This shouldn't have worried me, but it did. For some years past I had operated a scheme for dealing with Christmas. In October I'd begin writing cards for friends and family overseas, each eventually containing a personal letter – to be posted off in November. About then I'd begin buying presents for people I didn't expect to see over the actual holiday period. The people I knew I'd see on Christmas Eve, Christmas Day or in the week between Christmas and New Year, those closest to me, I'd buy for on Christmas Eve.

I know that most men and many women would consider shopping in central London on that day a peculiar kind of madness, but part of the ethos of Christmas, for me, is rushing between Hamleys – 'the largest toy shop in the world' – in Regent Street, John Lewis – 'never knowingly undersold' – in Oxford Street, and Harrod's in Knightsbridge. The streets are packed with people pushing and shoving, but for the most part in a good-natured way. There is a certain camaraderie about being in it together, at the last minute. All the shop windows are decorated, some gaudily, some tastefully. Every-thing is overpriced and much of it will inevitably end up reduced in the January sales, but there is still something magical about it, a vitality that I love being a part of. Well, I may have been forced to forego that particular delight this year, but I had not been idle. Determined to celebrate the Festive Season in the best way I knew how, I'd been making preparations.

I had for weeks been saving the inside sheets of the *Baghdad Observer*. By tearing the pages into strips and soaking them in water I found I had a very malleable papier mâché, and from this I had fashioned a small Christmas tree. Using the same material I had been able to decorate the tree with stars, bells, angels and balls. Beneath it were lumps of compressed paper I hoped looked like gifts waiting to be opened, and on the uppermost branch the traditional Christmas-tree fairy stood resplendent on one wobbly, grey, papier-mâché leg.

By carefully scanning every *Baghdad Observer* headline and tearing out the relevant letters, I had created my own festive message to myself. 'Merry Christmas' was spelled out above the washroom door in letters of varying shapes and sizes, glued there with the dreaded lentil soup I had known I must sometime, somehow, find a use for. As the sticky soup dried out, the letters fell to the floor, but each morning brought a new lentil glue supply, so this morning it was again complete.

Christmas Eve had brought an unexpected gift. I had almost despaired of finding a 'y' to end the word 'Merry': no headline seemed to contain the letter, and anything in smaller type would have looked stupid. Then, on Christmas Eve, I spotted it. In fact, it jumped off the page at me – the elusive 'y' I needed to complete my message was in the word 'Yugoslavia'. As I looked around I felt pleased with my effort. Of course, there were no traditional Christmas colours, no bright reds, whites or greens, everything was the same mush-grey, but I felt the decorations brightened up my cell enormously. It didn't seem incongruous to be singing carols today.

I was still singing when Hamid came past on his mid-morning inspection. He peered in through the hatch. The English lady was crazy! She had a paper tree with lumps of paper hanging from the branches – and what was that strung across the wall? Comprehension dawned; he laughed and called me to the hatch.

'You have shop,' he said with a wide grin. 'What can I buy?'

I hadn't expected to be able to laugh this Christmas Day, but suddenly I was laughing.

'Hamid, take it all, my paper tree, my soap, my home-made Scrabble set, my precious Christmas cake. All this can be yours for the key of my door. Everything I possess for my freedom. Take them, take them,' I giggled hysterically.

Hamid by now was looking concerned. Truly, he must have thought, the woman is going off her rocker. Not surprising really, shut up alone for months. On impulse he unlocked the cell door and handed me a blindfold. He steered me along the corridor, stopping at the door at the end. Taking a set of keys from a cupboard he selected one, opened the door and let me through.

'Take off your blindfold,' he instructed.

I stared in total disbelief. We were out on a rooftop terrace where sheer concrete walls rose to a height of about twenty feet. Across the top was stretched a large chunk of wire mesh through which I could see bright-blue sky.

'How wonderful!' I gasped.

Hamid smiled. 'Here you play for one half-hour. If you not like you knock on door.'

Was he crazy? There was no chance of that.

It is impossible to describe how marvellous it felt to be outside, to feel the sun on my face and to see that deep-blue cloudless sky above me. There were no windows in my cell. The only time I had ever been outside the prison walls was on the way to or from a meeting with Michelle or British Embassy officials, when I was always accompanied by guards, and, anyway, too preoccupied with immediate events to take in much of anything else. I had my peephole over the car park, but it was nothing like this. I walked around the perimeter of the terrace and looked up at the walls. There was nothing I could grip, no cracks or footholds, nothing but smooth, sheer concrete: the only way out of there would have been to sprout wings and fly. Still, I would make the most of it. I broke into a run, round and round, I went, head stretched back and arms flailing – it felt so great to be alive. How fantastic, how utterly fantastic! I slowed to a gentle jog and began to sing in time with the jogging.

> Jingle bells, jingle bells,
> Jingle all the way.
> Oh what fun it is to ride,
> On a one-horse open sleigh, oh!

Hamid looked through the peephole from the other side. Good, good, he must have said to himself, he'd warded off an imminent psychiatric attack. The English lady was happy again. Hamid prided himself on never having to hold down a prisoner for the medics to give their intravenous Valium. Oh no, not when he was in charge. He liked to keep his prisoners happy. Well, quite happy anyway.

Whatever his motives, he had given me the best Christmas present of my life and one I shall always remember. For a short space of time I felt free. I wasn't, but that's how it felt after four months in a windowless cell.

Christmas passed and New Year arrived. I had designed an invitation to put on the hatch door.

> You are invited to a New Year's Eve Party
> Everyone Welcome
> Food and Wine
> Music by the Boomtown Rats
>
> Bring a Bottle

Clinking champagne glasses and elegantly-dressed dancing couples gave the invitation a festive air. The guards came to look and smile and then they went away again.

New Year's Eve is a reflective time for many of us. Personally, I have found it can be depressing. I think that's why I love to get out and whoop it up; it helps keep the bogies away. I fell to thinking about my life. It's not been particularly unusual but, like everyone I guess, there have been ups and downs, rags to riches, riches to rags. In my late twenties, when I was with Cory, I'd lived like a queen, spending weeks sailing around exotic islands in our own boat, jetting off to the United States for a few action-packed days of shopping and night-life when the beauty and tranquillity of the Caribbean became too mundane for us. Only a few years later I was a single parent, struggling to raise a child on a nurse's salary, living from hand to mouth in a wet, windswept Berkshire village. Marriage to John brought nine years of comparative comfort and security – but if this cell was the wages of excitement, I could definitely live without it.

I stayed awake until 3 a.m., midnight at home in England. At one minute to three, I spooned dried milk into my cup, added the last of my coffee-grounds and mixed it with cold water. I held it aloft.

'Happy New Year Michelle. Happy New Year Martina, Erica, Joyce, Brenda, Alan. Happy New Year Anne, June, Janet, Gill, Joy. I'm thinking of you. I know you're thinking of me.' Tears fell into the cup.

On Twelfth Night I agonised over whether or not to take down the Christmas decorations which so brightened up my dismal cell. Superstition prevailed. More bad luck I could do without. Abdul Rahmed brought me a rubbish bag and, sadly, I dropped my paper treasures in.

Justice Will Be Done

Time passed slowly. The interrogations appeared to have ceased completely, and with Michelle's visit and Christmas behind me, there was nothing to look forward to. I intensified my keep-fit programme, stretching it out for many hours each day. My birthday came and went. There were no presents or cards – it was just another day.

Robin had said he would press for another meeting with me in January, but nothing happened. Without the interrogation sessions I had little contact with anyone other than the guards and the tea-boys. Abdullah, the guard from the hospital, came to see me a couple of times on so-called 'welfare visits'. I tried to find out whether or not I had been charged with any crime. He was able to tell me I was being held under Section 158, a legal statute pertaining to threats to Iraq's internal security, but he could not, or would not, say whether I was to be charged. I tried to quiz him on whether or not I would be represented by a lawyer, who that would be and how much it would cost my family. Again, I drew a complete blank – Abdullah could tell me nothing. I wondered what was happening to Farzad. He had made his confession video: was he now back in London, or still locked up somewhere in the interrogation centre, wondering, just as I was, what on earth was going to happen to us?

I spent hours at my cell hatch, like some lonely old lady behind her lace curtains, hoping to glimpse a familiar face or to overhear a few sentences of someone else's conversation. I heard Hamid speaking English to someone else further up the corridor. It might have been Farzad, it might not. No one seemed to know anything or, at least, no one was prepared to admit that they did.

January and most of February dragged interminably on in this way. They were the worst days and weeks I had known: long days and longer nights filled with frustration, anguish and sometimes overwhelming feelings of despair. I began to visualise myself alone in that single cell for ever. To commit someone to solitary confinement is surely the worst thing one human being can do to another. Gradually, stealthily and inevitably the victim is robbed of all sense of self. Sometimes I would crouch by the washroom tap, scrape out the loosely packed plaster and gaze through my tiny peephole at the outside world. With my face pressed to the dirty, slimy wall, I would remain there until my limbs were numb with cramp, watching the sky, the clouds, the car park and the activities of free men and women going about their everyday lives three storeys below.

Towards the end of February, after an interval of many weeks, I was taken down to the interrogation room. Here I was informed that I would soon go on trial.

'Tomorrow,' said the interrogator, 'you will see your lawyer.'

The following day, as always happened when anything unusual was scheduled to take place in my daily routine, I was woken at 6 a.m. I was to be taken to the Ministry of Foreign Affairs to meet the man who would represent me in court. Abdullah, who, I realised, had been allocated the job of my personal case worker, Abu Samir and two guards escorted me to the Ministry of Foreign Affairs. We arrived almost two hours before the meeting was due to take place. I was ushered into a fairly small room where I sat and waited while my escorts wandered in and out talking, laughing and drinking coffee. Just before 11 a.m. they settled down and we were joined by a man and a woman, presumably Ministry of Information observers, and Robin and Pauline. I didn't pay too much attention to the lawyer when he entered the room until I recognised a familiar voice saying, 'Hello, Dee!' To my amazement and delight it was my brother Alan who walked in behind him.

I had not been expecting a visit. I knew Michelle would not be coming to Baghdad in February and had resigned myself to the fact. Now, here was Alan. He smiled broadly and although touching between prisoners and visitors was absolutely forbidden, I was hugging him before anyone else in the room could utter a word to prevent it.

Alan is a few years older than me and when we were children he had to be the world's most horrible brother, playing the sort of tricks most people only read about in Enid Blyton stories. One of his favourites was to tie my long hair to the back of the chair at the breakfast table, so that when I got up my hair was almost dragged out of my head. Once he persuaded me to climb into a wheelbarrow, saying he would take me for a ride: the ride ended with him dumping me in a bed of stinging-nettles. Later, when I was in my teens and he was in his twenties, we became very close. Both single, we found there were many advantages in having a presentable partner for parties and dances. Now Alan had become a respectable computer consultant with a family.

The lawyer didn't look Iraqi. With his light-brown, almost sandy hair he could have been Turkish or Syrian. My spirits rose: if I had a foreign lawyer surely he was much less likely to be a puppet of the Iraqi regime. Maybe I would get a reasonably fair trial after all. Unfortunately, it took only minutes for optimism to give way to disappointment as the lawyer fended off my questions.

'Would you give me some idea of how I can best present my case?' I asked.

In response he smiled enigmatically and murmured, 'Justice will be done.'

'What is going to happen to me? I am not a spy, nor am I against the State. How should I explain this to the court?'

'Justice will be done,' he again intoned.

Was this man a lunatic? I wondered. Is that how they were

proposing to get me imprisoned, by giving me a complete nut-case for a lawyer? To each question I put to him the response was the same: 'Justice will be done.' Well, I had already had a taste of Iraqi justice and had less faith in it than this affable advocate appeared to.

I felt Alan might, as a man, have more success with the lawyer. Although women play a very important part in Iraqi life both at home and in the work-force, the society is still very much a male-dominated one. But it didn't work that way. Neither Alan nor Robin were able to make any headway.

The interrogators had made quite an issue out of my remark to Farzad that I 'carry a camera all the time'. I was anxious to know if there were any rules governing the carrying or use of a camera in Iraq. The extent of his legal advice on this point was: 'You have nothing to worry about.'

Robin asked him three times what I was being charged with, but he was unable or unwilling to say. It was hopeless and apart from the joy of seeing Alan, I felt the whole meeting had been a waste of everybody's time. However, it did make us confident that the court case was imminent and Alan assured me he would remain in Iraq until it was all over.

I spent the next few days preparing my case: since I had no confidence in the lawyer chosen for me, I would just have to do the best I could on my own. I went over the details of our visits to Hilla again and again in my mind, recalling all the questions the interrogators had put to me, preparing myself for the sort of stiff cross-examinations I had been getting at the interrogation centre. I had no experience of courts at all – I have never even been called for jury service – but I was determined I would give this my very best shot. I was not guilty of any crime and the court must be made to see that. I must be found not guilty. The alternative was too awful to contemplate.

On the morning of the trial I was woken at 6.30 a.m. and told to dress. Two hours passed before I was taken to a van without windows and only a narrow shelf, which passed for a seat. Abu Samir and two guards accompanied me. Attempting to hang on to the sides of the van as we bumped along, I was also trying to peep through the curtain that separated me from the driver. I saw that we were on the road to Fallugia, which was later bombed by British pilots during the Gulf War. The van pulled up outside the Revolutionary Court building and let us out before driving away.

We stood only a few feet from a large dark-coloured car. In the back seat, a guard on either side, sat Farzad. So, he had not been allowed to return home, despite his confession. I wondered how making the video would affect his chances of a fair trial. I could see from his face alone that he had lost weight, he was hollow-cheeked and even more gaunt-looking than when we had last met. We looked at each other and each of us saw the unspoken prayer in the other's eyes: 'Please God, let common sense prevail and set us free.'

But there would be no decision made about our freedom today. As we hung about, waiting anxiously for some sign that the proceedings were about to begin, someone came out of the building and told the guards that our trial had been postponed. Clearly there had been a simple breakdown in communications, but after all the anticipation and anguish, to hear the news that the trial would not now go ahead today was sickeningly disappointing. How much longer could this go on? Finally, I was put into the front seat of the car in which Farzad was held. He was furious.

'Fucking assholes!' he yelled, anger and pent-up frustration blazing out of his black eyes. 'Why didn't they tell us in advance? If there was a World Cup for inefficiency, Iraq would win it.'

'*Hallas!*' shouted the guard, meaning 'Finish! Shut up!'

Over the car radio came a football-match commentary in Arabic; the driver and guards appeared engrossed. I began to sing, softly, to the tune of 'Baa, Baa Black Sheep'.

> What is going to happen to us?
> Have you been charged yet?
> I am being held under Section 158.

Farzad took over.

> If you are released and
> Get back to the UK,
> Go and see a friend of mine
> Who lives in Camberley.

It made no sense to me at all, but he continued to sing the street and the number of the house he wanted me to visit should I be released before him. Meanwhile, the driver and the guards argued over the various merits of the football teams that were playing. No one appeared to notice what we were doing.

The trial was rescheduled for 8 March, ten days away. When I returned to my cell I scratched ten marks on the wall, and crossed off one of them every evening before settling down on the mattress to sleep. They were the longest ten days of my life. I had gone over my account of what happened repeatedly until it had almost ceased to make sense to me. I was suffering from acute tension which no amount of yoga could dissipate. My lower lip and left thumb went numb and my mind refused to concentrate on even the most menial of tasks: for example, I would look down and discover that I was wearing only one sock.

Eventually the day arrived when we were taken back to the Revolutionary Court building. Inside we were ushered into a large waiting-room filled with row after row of slatted wooden seats. Farzad was put in the front row and I in the back. Another prisoner, wearing blue-and-white-striped pyjamas and flip-flops, was sitting somewhere around the middle section. It was like being on the top deck of a jumbo-sized bus, while Abu Samir and four armed guards walked up and down the aisle.

About an hour passed before we were called into the courtroom and led up two steps into the dock, which was a rectangular-shaped wooden pen, approximately 12 feet by 4 feet in size. Three generals sat opposite, dressed in full military uniform; a clerk sat on a table to our left. I was in the middle of the dock, Farzad stood to my right and the unknown prisoner in the pyjamas to my left. A door in the courtroom opened to admit my lawyer and two other men, I assumed also lawyers, who approached the bench and bowed to the judge before sitting at a long desk opposite the clerk. Robin Kealy brought up the rear. He was seated in a plain wooden chair close to the lawyers. It was comforting to have Robin nearby, albeit as a passive observer. It certainly made me feel that we were not entirely alone in this mess.

The trial began. The entire proceedings were conducted in Arabic and I waited in vain for someone to translate into English what was being said in the courtroom, for someone to tell me what was happening. I hadn't the faintest idea of what was being said. No translation was given as my lawyer read out a long statement: the only words he spoke in my defence that I actually understood were my own name. He had never discussed his defence strategy with me, never really asked me any questions, so I had no notion of what he was talking about. I strongly suspected that he didn't have a great deal more.

After the lawyers had had their say, Farzad was called to speak. My heart sank as I realised Abu Samir was translating. Farzad began by stating that he was a journalist with the *Observer*, but that he also did freelance reporting, particularly for a Scottish newspaper. I listened with growing concern as he went on to describe in detail a holiday he had recently spent in Germany. The things he was saying to the court about his time in Germany seemed to me totally irrelevant. Why on earth should anyone here want to know who picked him up and dropped him off at the airport? Speaking with barely a pause for breath, he continued with his rambling yarn, giving unnecessary details about his life at home. Abu Samir tried unsuccessfully to get him back on the right track. 'Keep to the point,' he rapped. 'Make your sentences short.' But it was to no avail; Farzad continued just as before.

After an hour or so I was fed up with this seemingly endless flow of useless information. I told myself to be tolerant: Farzad was entitled to use any method he wished in order to plead his case, but it was difficult to understand how boring the judges into a coma would achieve that.

Farzad was now retracting the so-called 'confession' that had been shown on Iraqi television, claiming that he had made it under pressure. 'I was a frightened man,' he said.

I hadn't believed it anyway. After all, I had been sorely tempted to give false information because of my fear of the interrogators and also, amazing as it now seems, in exchange for milk and fruit.

'I feel relaxed here,' Farzad interjected from time to time, making me wonder if perhaps he had been given a shot of Valium or something similar earlier that morning. He was back in full flow again. It was as if he was on stage giving a well-rehearsed performance of an obscure play that nobody could understand. It wasn't just me; looking around the court it was clear that everyone was baffled. Our fidgeting was finally interrupted by Robin Kealy, who stood up and made a statement to the effect that the British Embassy had not, under any circumstances, agreed to send Farzad's soil samples through the diplomatic bag. Following Robin's announcement, Abu Samir swiftly turned the questioning to me. I had often thought he had aspirations to become an interrogator; today he was in his element playing at being a lawyer.

'Are you guilty or innocent?' he barked at me.

'Innocent or guilty of what?' I asked. 'As far as I know I haven't been charged with an offence.'

This seemed to cause quite a stir in the court. Abu Samir repeated the question. 'You must answer innocent or guilty.'

'Then I shall answer innocent, since I have not done any-thing which could be described as guilty.'

I had been bitterly disappointed when I saw that Abu Samir was to act as interpreter at these proceedings, but as he began to harangue me in the same old way I felt the tension disappear. This was familiar ground to me by now: it was Dee versus Abu Samir rather than the might of the Iraqi legal system.

'You are not new to Iraq,' he continued with a sneer. 'You must know the circumstances our country is in. The war with

Iran is not yet settled, yet you have deliberately helped an expatriate to collect information from a military area.'

I replied that I had arrived in Iraq in August 1988 after the cease-fire had been agreed with Iran. I had no experience of the war.

'Why did you agree to go to Hilla with Bazoft using a hospital car?'

'The car I used was not a hospital car as such. It was an ordinary four-wheel-drive vehicle for the use of staff when they were off duty.'

'But not for Bazoft's use,' Abu Samir shot back.

'The cars are for the use of hospital staff and their friends. I did not need permission to take Farzad as a passenger. My only requirement was to log my route with the transport office in the hospital, which I did.'

'But you knew Bazoft was planning to take photographs?'

'No, but having said that, I assume that if you allow journalists to bring cameras into the country, you also allow them to use them. There were no notices at Hilla to say that photography was forbidden. Is there a law here which states that I cannot take into my car a person carrying a camera?'

'There would be no problem about taking a photograph of Babylon, but using a camera in a secret location is unacceptable.'

'But we didn't go into the secret location. It was fenced off. I told Farzad there was to be no fence-climbing and he agreed. We simply drove along the outside of the wire fence and it was there, outside of the wire fence, that we saw what looked like coal-dust, piled up on the side of the road. I, personally, didn't think it could come from the explosion site because, although I am not a chemist, I would have thought that explosive waste would be toxic and, therefore, dangerous. In which case it wouldn't be left lying by the side of the road.'

'What happened to the soil samples?'

'Farzad told me that he had taken them to the British Embassy to ask if they could be put into the diplomatic bag. He also said the Embassy had refused his request.'

'Have you anything else to say to the court?'

'I don't know what I'm supposed to be defending myself against. What exactly am I guilty of?'

'How can you pretend you are innocent?' asked Abu Samir with disdain.

The questioning moved to the unknown prisoner on my left and was conducted in Arabic, so at the end of it I was none the wiser. I didn't know the man and had no idea why he was being tried with us, but he was clearly implicated in some way.

Shortly afterwards we were led from the courtroom and told the trial would continue in two days.

That evening Abdullah came to my cell door bearing gifts of milk and cheese.

'I brought these from a nearby hotel,' he said with a look of genuine warmth and kindness on his face.

'Thank you, Abdullah, you are very kind.' I wished I could feel the same warmth towards him as I did to Hamid, the English-speaking guard who had taken me on to the rooftop terrace on Christmas Day and sprayed my cell, against his better judgement, to get rid of the cockroaches. Unfortunately, every time I saw Abdullah, with his tufts of facial hair and his narrowed eyes, I was reminded of the way he would follow us around the hospital, noting everything we said and did to report back to his secret police taskmasters. But perhaps with those very connections he might know more about what was currently happening than I did. It was worth a try.

'Abdullah, can you help me? I still don't know why I am here. It seems an awful lot of fuss about a bit of ash.'

Abdullah thought for a moment. 'Perhaps Allah has put you here to prevent you being knocked down and killed in a car accident.'

I shuddered. Was he trying to tell me I was lucky to be alive?

Day Two of the trial was a repeat of Day One, except that it was much shorter. The generals talked among themselves for a few minutes and everyone stood up. This was it, the dreaded moment when we discovered what our fate was to be. We, too, stood up. It was impossible for me to gauge the mood of the generals from the faces around me. My brother Alan was not in court; I later learned he had been forbidden to attend. Robin Kealy had not looked at either Farzad or myself once during the course of the trial. I knew he spoke fluent Arabic and would have welcomed some signal of support at that moment, but none was forthcoming. I had come to regard Robin as a friend and his behaviour, his refusal to acknowledge either myself or Farzad with even a glance, was confusing and distressing to me. Involuntarily I clenched and unclenched my hands. My mouth was dry and I could feel my legs shaking uncontrollably. I glanced at Farzad: there seemed to be a slight nervous tick working beneath his right eye. Abu Samir stared at me impassively while the sentences were read out in Arabic and his expression remained completely blank as he motioned us to leave the dock. We trooped outside to the waiting-area and sat down on the slatted wooden benches. I looked at Farzad. He was as white as a sheet.

'Did the judge say he was going to hang me?' he croaked.

Abu Samir laughed out loud. 'No, no, the judge said he was not going to hang you.'

'What about me?' I asked. 'What did the judge say about me?'

'It hasn't been decided yet,' Abu Samir said. 'When they are quite ready the sentences will be typed up and sent to the interrogation centre.'

I didn't believe him, not for a minute. Why wouldn't he tell me what had been said? It had been a trial and we had been sentenced. My fate and Farzad's had been decided in that courtroom and we had a right to know.

'But I need to know what was said,' I persisted. 'Am I going to be released or what?'

'Who knows? Maybe you will get a little sentence. Maybe not.'

Why wouldn't Abu Samir tell us what was going on? Our sentences had obviously been decided and announced in open court. He knew perfectly well what was going to happen. How typical of him!

We all drove back to the interrogation centre in the same

car. The journey was made in silence. Farzad stared straight ahead blankly; he could have been in another world.

Abu Samir got out of the car as it stopped just inside the entrance of the interrogation centre and walked away, leaving Farzad and me with two guards. The driver drove the car away, into the covered car park. One of the guards went with him. Farzad and I were now left alone with one guard, who walked slowly across to a prefabricated hut close by. As we watched, he put his hands on either side of the door-frame and stuck his head inside to talk to someone. It was clearly someone he knew well, because soon we could hear loud talking and laughter. There were no windows on the side of the hut, so the guard was unable to see what we were doing. It seemed incredible: we stood there just inside the entrance of the interrogation centre, only yards from the road where ordinary Baghdadis were going about their daily business, unguarded and unobserved.

'Farzad,' I said quickly. 'It would be easy for you to escape. You could make a run for it.' He didn't look at me or answer. I knew that being female with fair hair, blue eyes and dressed the way I was, I hadn't a hope of losing myself in the crowds thronging the pavements a few yards away from where we stood. But Farzad could do it. He was dressed in a dark blazer and grey trousers, as were dozens of the Iraqi men walking about the streets just beyond the gate.

'No one is watching, Farzad. It would be easy,' I urged, unable to bear the thought of him being locked up for perhaps twenty years. He wasn't registering what I was saying. His eyes were glazed over as if he was in shock; he appeared to be rooted to the spot, unable to move. I almost felt like pushing him towards the road.

'Farzad!' I hissed. But he was out of my reach, somewhere miles away. I noticed that he jumped and looked startled when the guard returned to us a few moments later.

We went inside the building. I was told to wait with the guard who was seated at a desk just inside the door. Another guard escorted Farzad to the lift. As the doors closed, he was staring out like someone in a dream. I waved, but he didn't respond. It was the last time I saw him alive.

I didn't sleep at all that night. If only I spoke better Arabic, so that I'd have understood the sentences for myself! There had been no clues. Robin's face had given nothing away when the court had stood for the judge to pass the sentences, and he had left fairly hurriedly, looking neither right nor left. What was it Abu Samir had said to me? 'Maybe you will get a little sentence, maybe not.'

In my desperation I managed to persuade myself that I had been let off. What else could it be? Abu Samir had been telling me for five months that if I didn't cooperate with him and confess, I would spend the rest of my days in prison. Now that I had been found not guilty he didn't want to be the one to tell me: it would be humiliating for him to lose face. I began fantasising. Would I go back to the hospital or would I be sent home? When was the next flight to London? There was probably one every day, I thought. Would I be able to get a job? Then I pulled myself up short. Here I was, wondering about flying home and finding a job and I hadn't a clue what was going to happen to Farzad. Was it possible that he, too, had been let off? Perhaps Abu Samir wanted to keep him squirming on the hook a little longer too?

We hadn't done anything really wrong, for Heaven's sake! What was a bit of ash that had been left lying on the roadside? All right, he probably shouldn't have asked the British Embassy to put it in the diplomatic bag – but in any case, they had refused.

As the night wore on I made several cups of cold coffee, using water from the washroom tap. I didn't need to ration the milk powder any more. How wonderful it was going to be to switch on an electric kettle and make a decent cup of tea, to walk around my London flat, sleep in a bed, sit on a chair, eat at a table. Roast lamb – I would have roast lamb with mint sauce and all the trimmings. For months I had been fantasising about sitting down to a meal of roast lamb: on numerous occasions I saw the plate before me in a dream. Surely the dream would now come true at last, and I'd be reunited with my family. They probably knew the verdict already, I thought. I was, of course, deluding myself: dawn brought a very different reality from the one I had envisaged.

I was jolted awake from a light sleep at 6 a.m. by Bad News yelling that I should get dressed. Usually it was the rattle of the tea-trolley that acted as my alarm call. Despite the urgency in his voice, it was not until two hours later that he returned.

'*Yalla!*' he roared. I went with him to the ground floor of the building and out into the car park to the hut where Dr Raad and I had parted company when I'd been arrested six months before. A guard sitting at a rickety table handed me an envelope containing my watch and keys, and produced a book for me to sign. I didn't know if he spoke English, but I asked anyway, 'Where am I going?'

He looked up at me and shook his head. 'I not know. You ask another.'

I was escorted out of the room and into what appeared to be a sort of rest-room for the guards. A few of them sat around on beat-up or broken chairs, passing around a jam-jar filled with black tea.

'Where am I going?' I asked them, first in English and then in Arabic. No one answered, no one even looked at me. I banged my fist on the table and repeated the question in a sharper, louder voice. 'Where am I going?'

'You go to British Embassy,' said one of the guards.

To the Embassy? Were they letting me go today? If I was going to the Embassy, they must be. I was going to be free. I threw my arms around the guard and kissed his cheek. 'Thank you, thank you, oh, thank you so much!' I kissed them all, grinned like a Cheshire cat and went around them all again shaking their hands. They bundled me into a car, and I shouted and waved like a gleeful child as we sped away. Away from six months of isolation and loneliness, away from the ants, the cockroaches, away from lentil soup. I threw myself back into the car seat and gazed out of the window. I felt relieved, elated, wonderful. My ordeal was finally over. I looked at the trees and the blue sky with delight and found new appreciation in them. I was free!

After a time I began to look around more objectively. Which road was this? We passed a group of buildings I didn't recognise and my stomach lurched. This wasn't a route I had ever taken, and I considered I knew Baghdad well. Something was wrong, and surely the sun should be on the other side! We were travelling south, but why? The British Embassy should be to the north-west.

'Where are we going?' I asked quietly.

The guard travelling with me in the front of the car appeared to understand my broken Arabic. He picked up a letter from the seat beside him and waved it in my direction, saying something about having to drop it off at a friend's house. I didn't allow myself to think anything. I made my mind a total blank. They had told me I was going to the British Embassy and although I knew the Embassy was not in this direction, if I stayed quiet and still and didn't antagonise anyone, eventually we would arrive there. The alternative – that I wasn't going to the Embassy – was too horrible to contemplate.

A few miles down the road the car stopped. The guard got out of the car and I watched him give the letter to a young man. So far, so good. The car started up again, but instead of turning round, we continued to travel southwards. Now what? I pictured Robin and Pauline waiting for me in the Embassy. I imagined my arrival there. If only I had some clean clothes! I craned my head to look in the car mirror and saw myself for the first time in six months. I hardly recognised my own face. My skin was a pale greenish-grey. My hair looked like a ball of wool that had been massacred by a group of kittens. My blue eyes stared back at me, dull and lifeless and surrounded by black circles. I sniffed and wondered if I also smelled. I looked like someone who would smell. Still, I would soon be able to enjoy the luxury of a hot bath with bubbles and thick towels to dry myself on. Perhaps Pauline would have some make-up I could borrow, and maybe I could go to the Melia Hotel for a cut and blow-dry.

We were turning off the main road, passing marshland and an army firing range, heading for a large gate set into a high wall with several strands of barbed wire stretched across the top. Two soldiers with guns stepped forward to check a number of documents the guard was holding through the car window. The gates swung open, we drove through them into a dusty, walled yard and stopped in front of a prefabricated building.

'*Yalla!*' The guard beckoned me. I got out of the car and followed him into the building. We sat down on a wooden bench.

A man in a brown Crimplene suit entered the room from another door and indicated that I should go with him. I stood up and looked around, but the guard from the interrogation centre had left without a word. I followed the man with the brown suit into another room where three men sat behind a long table arranged, like an office desk, with files, a telephone and piles of papers scattered about.

'Does anyone here speak English?' I asked in Arabic.

They shook their heads. I sat down, numb with fear. I simply didn't understand what was happening. Surely the guards at the interrogation centre wouldn't have told me I was going to the British Embassy as a joke? It would be too cruel. They had seen how delighted I was. Could it be possible that they had invented the story? No, this was probably some sort of process that had to be gone through before I was released. There were probably papers to sign, or release documents to be issued. It was just the Iraqis and their endless bureaucracy again. Suddenly that explanation didn't make any sense either. Why bring me so far out of Baghdad just to sign a few papers?

This went on for about half an hour without me getting any closer to an answer. I was still silently debating with myself when a female guard entered the room. She was quite young, stocky but pretty. She smiled and said, 'Hello, how are you?'

By now I was much too agitated to observe any social niceties. 'Where am I? What is this place?' I stammered.

The smile never left her face as she said, 'You are in prison.'

'In prison? I should be at the British Embassy. There must be some mistake. In prison? I don't understand. For how long?'

She leaned across the desk and nonchalantly flicked through a file. 'Fifteen years.'

I think my heart stopped beating, then restarted and jumped up into my throat. My head was spinning, I felt weak and cold. Dozens of minuscule droplets of sweat formed on my brow; I felt them trickle down my face and watched them fall into my lap. Fifteen years! Fifteen years! I'd be an old woman by the time I was released and Michelle would be thirty-six. My God – Michelle – did she know what had happened? I couldn't bear to think of the pain the knowledge would bring her. She had been so brave and such a source of support. And what of Farzad? If I had been sentenced to fifteen years, what would they do to him?

A Toast To Freedom

The telephone rang at 9 a.m. on 10 March. It was Stephen Lamport, an official from the Foreign Office who had been dealing with my mother's case.

'I'm afraid the news is not good, Michelle,' he said quietly. 'The trial only lasted for half an hour this morning and the sentences were harsh. Your mother, I'm sorry to say, has been given a fifteen-year sentence and Farzad has been condemned to execution.'

I heard myself scream out loud. My legs seemed to give way and as I sat down and tried to speak I realised I was babbling in a confused, demented sort of way, making no sense even to myself. Peter, on hearing my scream, came into the room and held my hand. I continued to listen to Stephen's words, but my mind was in a whirl.

'Obviously our priority is to have Farzad's sentence commuted, although we have made it absolutely clear to the Iraqis what we think about their decision. Their Ambassador has been summoned to the Foreign Office and we are trying to arrange for the Foreign Secretary, Douglas Hurd, to fly to Baghdad to deliver our sentiments personally to Saddam Hussein. If you would like to come along to the Foreign Office to discuss what action you would like to see taken, please feel free to do so at any time.'

I replaced the receiver, too confused and sickened to consider what my next move should be. Peter put his arms around me. 'Those bastards, those bastards,' he kept repeating.

It took a few minutes to pull myself together. I realised that it could only be a matter of time before the Press got hold of the news and it suddenly seemed very urgent that I be the one to tell our relatives and my mother's friends what the latest development was. I didn't want any eager young reporter breaking this sort of news to them. I made a lot of calls and listened to a lot of good sense from worried friends and relatives. They were right, it wasn't over yet, not by a long way, and I was determined to do everything I possibly could to see that the Iraqis realised what a dreadful mistake they had made.

The second telephone call that morning was from Foreign Office Minister William Waldegrave, who expressed his shock at the sentences and reiterated that the British Government would be doing everything in its power to stop Farzad's execution. Immediately after replacing the receiver I began getting enquiries from the Press. 'When did I hear? How did I feel? Who had I spoken to?' I must have spoken to a hundred journalists all wanting to know the same things. I could understand how they felt: as well as this being a story, Farzad was one of them. Their interest and concern was natural enough, but I couldn't spend all my time on the telephone. I decided to hold a press conference. I contacted a television journalist friend of mine, Jon Scammell, who spoke to colleagues at Associated Press and arranged for a statement to be put out to newsrooms all over the country, stating where and when we were holding it.

Donald Trelford, the Editor of the *Observer*, had agreed to allow me to use a room in the newspaper building. When I arrived there with Peter and Jon at 4.30 p.m. there were about nine camera crews waiting outside the entrance to the building, each of them desperate to get an exclusive story. Jon ushered me inside and Donald spent a few moments advising me on how to approach my first press conference.

I entered the conference room to find it packed to the doors with reporters; they looked as if they were standing on each other's heads. In addition to about 150 journalists there were cameramen, sound men and photographers. I was shaking like a leaf. Jon addressed the reporters first.

'Michelle will be making a statement first and then if you would like to ask her some questions, she will take one from each of you.'

I looked up nervously and tried to focus my mind on what I was going to say.

'This is my first press conference,' I began. 'I'm extremely nervous, so you will have to be patient with me. But before I begin to read my statement, I would ask you all to be very careful when reporting this issue in tomorrow's papers. The situation is now so sensitive that any over-zealous reporting that might upset the Iraqi Government will not help our primary concerns, which as you all know is to have Farzad's sentence commuted and my mother's dropped.' I then began my statement.

It is grossly unfair and justice has not been done today. Having heard of the evidence that my mother gave in court on Thursday, it is clear to me that she is guilty of nothing as I have maintained all along. I have been to the Foreign Office today and they have assured me that they will be protesting in the strongest possible manner. I sincerely hope that President Saddam Hussein of Iraq will not allow this miscarriage of justice. I am told that the sentences cannot be carried out until he has agreed to them. I would plead with him to intervene. My whole family cannot believe what has happened this morning in Iraq. I know that I have said this before, but it is important for me to stress that my mother is a nurse and has never been a spy, and that they did not go inside this restricted zone. My mother's only crime – if it is a crime – was to drive to the perimeter fence. For her to spend fifteen years in an Iraqi prison for simply doing that does not make sense.

Immediately after I had finished, cameras began to flash from every angle as questions were fired at me.

'Will you be going to Baghdad?'

'What has the Foreign Office told you?'

'Have you been able to speak to your mother today?'

Questions, questions and more questions. I spent about half an hour trying to answer them, which seemed to go very quickly. Then there were a few more photographs before Jon Scammel intervened. 'I think that's enough for now,' he told his colleagues from newspapers, radio and television. 'If you would kindly let Michelle leave, I think she should be allowed some peace and quiet for the rest of the day.'

By the time I returned home half an hour later there were forty-two messages on my answering machine and the telephone didn't stop ringing after that.

The news in England was dominated by the sentence. Farzad's photograph was flashed across the screen that night and the press conference was relayed to the nation. The phone continued to ring every two minutes or so throughout the night as friends and well-wishers expressed their shock. We took 230 calls from people in the media who wanted television, radio and newspaper interviews.

The following morning I was up at 6 a.m. to appear on TV AM with Donald Trelford and then off to do an interview with BBC Television, via Sky Television and GLR Radio. I was determined to get across the message that Farzad and my mother should be released to as many people as possible and this seemed an efficient way of achieving just that. At midday I joined a protest outside the

Iraqi Embassy in London, where journalists and friends of Farzad held a silent demonstration, holding photographs and drawings of him. Donald Trelford handed a letter to the Iraqi Ambassador who, it appears, had received seven hundred telephone calls from members of the public protesting at the sentences.

The Government was also quick off the mark, as Foreign Office Minister William Waldegrave had promised it would be. The Iraqi Ambassador was summoned to the Foreign Office and was told that Britain would be appealing against the harsh sentences passed on Farzad and my mother on humanitarian grounds. The Government would also be asking the United Nations and the European Community for their Support. Foreign Secretary Douglas Hurd announced he would lead a delegation to Iraq in an attempt to overturn the death sentence on Farzad and to gain a reduced sentence for my mother. Prime Minister Margaret Thatcher said in a statement that she was 'horrified' and 'would be appealing to Saddam Hussein for clemency on humanitarian grounds'. Mrs Thatcher also enlisted the help of King Hussein of Jordan, who was at the time visiting Britain with his wife, Queen Noor. A valued friend of Iraq, the King of Jordan said he would attempt to get Saddam Hussein to change his mind. The governments of countries around the world spoke out against the sentences. There was genuine outrage.

It was a race to save Farzad's life, for no one had any indication if or when his sentence would be carried out. Under the Iraqi 'judicial' system there is no such thing as an appeal court, so once sentence has been passed there is little cause for delay. Since only President Saddam Hussein could commute the sentences, it was necessary not to anger him in any way. It was not easy, but many times during television and radio interviews I had to praise Iraq and thank the President. It was always through gritted teeth and with clenched hands, but if it helped to get Farzad and my mother home, it seemed a small price to pay.

I managed to arrange a meeting with the Iraqi Ambassador to give him a letter expressing my personal horror at the turn of events. During a meeting lasting about half an hour, I pleaded with him to help get Farzad's sentence reduced. He seemed genuinely sympathetic and assured me he would do what he could. Although he gave the impression of being a kindly old soul, he seemed somewhat weak and pathetic and I doubted that he had any real influence. Whether or not he conveyed any of our conversation to Saddam Hussein I never discovered.

I was exhausted, living off nervous energy, unable to eat or sleep. I did interview after interview, knowing it was a race against time. I wrote a personal letter to the Ambassador or High Commissioner of every foreign embassy in London. 'If you feel that you would be able to win justice for my mother and Farzad Bazoft, please lend your support to my campaign,' I concluded each letter. More than thirty ambassadors responded. I also wrote letters to the *Independent* newspaper asking the general public to join our campaign, but despite more than one thousand letters and five petitions containing thousands of names to the Iraqis, Saddam Hussein remained unmoved, stating that he would not be forced into 'acting under pressure'.

The Iraqi News Agency, INA, quoting an Iraqi Foreign Ministry spokesman, said that the British reaction to the sentence was 'hasty' and that President Saddam Hussein 'could not intervene while under political pressure'. By this time over twenty countries had deplored the sentence, including some thought to be among Iraq's strongest allies. The European Community drafted a motion asking its members to isolate Iraq if it carried out its threat to execute Farzad. It seemed the whole world was fighting to save him, but Saddam Hussein was ignoring their efforts and there had been no official reaction from the Iraqi Government. British Prime Minister Margaret Thatcher had had no response to her personal request to Baghdad nor, it seemed, had any other world leader. And all those involved were aware that in this case no news was bad news.

I went to the Foreign Office where I met William Waldegrave. He confirmed what I had suspected: 'The situation is extremely sensitive at the moment and the Press are not helping matters.' It was true: the newspapers, in a mixture of outraged horror, indignation, belligerence and genuine sympathy for the plights of Farzad, an ordinary British journalist in Iraq doing his job, and my mother, an ordinary British nurse doing a friend a favour, had taken the story to their hearts. They were carrying articles about Saddam Hussein's appalling human-rights record, as well as accounts of countless atrocities committed by him and catalogued by members of Iraqi political opposition parties in exile. While I didn't doubt for a second that every word of what they wrote was absolutely true, I knew that headlines such as 'The Butcher of Baghdad', relayed from the Iraqi Embassy in London to the Gulf as fast as modern technology could carry them, were not in any way helping our campaign.

Outside the Foreign Office I gave an informal press conference to about twenty journalists waiting there. I told them just what William Waldegrave had said and added, 'He promised that the Government are doing all they can. We still believe that Farzad can be saved, but I would plead with you to resist the temptation of using adjectives such as "brutal" and "barbaric" when mentioning the Iraqi President. We really need to keep him sweet at the moment.'

After leaving the Foreign Office I did an interview for Sky Television and later, during the afternoon, several radio broadcasts from the flat. I wanted to get through as much as possible during the day, since I had promised myself I would take the evening off. There was to be a party at a Battersea restaurant for Julia, one of my best friends, who was celebrating her birthday. There were people at the party I hadn't seen for years, and while most of the evening was spent bringing friends up to date on events, I was able to put the main issue out of my mind for a few hours. We all drank a toast to Julia and then, passing me the cork from the champagne bottle, she said, 'This is for you, Michelle, it's good luck. Now let's drink a toast to freedom, for Dee and Farzad.' I raised my glass.

At home, I placed the 'lucky' cork on the shelf above my bed.

Tell Dee I'm Sorry

Fifteen years – I couldn't believe it. I was led away from the office in a daze.

A female guard told me in broken English that she was taking me to see Mohammed, who was in charge of the prison. I took an instant dislike to this man. He spoke a little English, but not enough to enable him to complete the regulation forms on new arrivals. I did my best to answer his halting questions, but the exercise was unsuccessful. Mohammed threw his pen down in exasperation, tossed the incomplete forms into an already bulging drawer and slammed it shut. Looking at the way they handled the paperwork in this place I didn't fancy my chances of early parole.

Mohammed flung open the door and called to a passing female guard, who glared at me with obvious contempt. She reminded me of a Boxer dog a former neighbour of ours once kept, but I suspected that unlike the dog, this woman didn't have a good side. '*Yalla*,' she said. I followed her along the corridor, beneath a wooden archway and through a metal gate. On the other side of the gate women covered from head to toe in long black gowns were packed shoulder to shoulder. It was a frightening experience trying to get through the teeming mass of bodies, a bit like trying to fight your way through a huge flock of crows. I was reminded of the Alfred Hitchcock film *The Birds*.

As we jostled our way through, hands reached out to touch my hair. I tossed my head and glared at the women around me

– they had better not try that again. Rounding a corner we were forced to wade through a stretch of dark-brown mud before reaching a concrete area containing five open cesspits. The stench of excrement pounded through my nostrils, making me feel light-headed and nauseous. We approached a doorway set in a single-storey L-shaped building. I hung back, reluctant to discover what was inside. But the ever-helpful female guard was there with a friendly shove of encouragement which sent me whirling through the door, over a rough stone step and into a cell.

The first thing I noticed was a pair of garish pink nylon curtains hanging at a window criss-crossed with stout iron bars. Three iron beds and mattresses lined the square room, which was about the size of a single bedroom. I peered around. Four pairs of eyes stared back at me from the mattress on the floor. A dark-haired, very pale-skinned woman of about thirty stood up and extended her hand. She was wholesome-looking, with a square face and a caring expression. I felt an immediate empathy with her.

'Welcome,' she said in English. 'My name is Nisreen. This is Sabiha,' she said, pointing to a girl of about twenty with dark skin and glittering black eyes. 'This is Tanya.' She indicated an even younger girl with European features and light-brown hair. 'And,' she laughed, 'you won't be able to pronounce the name, so call this one Ann.' She pointed to a middle-aged woman with a placid face and spreading hips.

'None of them speak English. How is your Arabic?'

'Woefully inadequate, I'm afraid.' Even if no one else in the entire prison spoke English, at least I had found one person who did.

'How long have you been here, Nisreen?'

'Five years, but it seems longer.'

'What do you do all day?'

'Nothing very much. We sleep a lot, we eat, we talk and in the evening when it's cooler, we walk a little outside, and, of course, we pray.'

Still marvelling not so much at what Nisreen said but at the fact that she was saying it in English, I sat down on one of the

beds, but stood up immediately when I spotted Sabiha's
scowl. My goodness, she looked a bad-tempered girl.

'Do you read books?' I asked Nisreen.

'No, books are not allowed here, except for the Koran, of
course.'

'Are you allowed to write letters?'

'No. Pens and paper are now allowed either. We are
expected to sit on our beds and repent. The days are very
long.'

On hearing a stifled giggle I turned around to find the open
doorway crammed with faces. Old faces, young faces, some
with no teeth, others with beaming smiles.

'Hello, hello!' they chorused.

One of the women came into the room holding out a plate
of chicken and rice. It smelled delicious, but more than that, I
was being offered something by one of these women; I was
being presented with a gift.

During the months I'd spent in solitary confinement I had
often wondered what it would be like to be in a prison with
others. Sometimes I felt the presence of other women might be
horribly intrusive, all speaking Arabic and, as likely as not,
despising me for my Western-ness. At other times I longed for
company so much the devil himself would have been a
welcome cell guest. Now, here I was among them, my dream/
nightmare come true. I was speaking English and being
offered food. No more trying to peer out of the hatch of my
cell, no more straining my ears for the sound of the trolley,
which for six months had been the only measurement of time I
had known.

I sat on the floor and took a few mouthfuls of the chicken
before I realised that I was crying. This pattern was to repeat
itself for two days. Each time a plate of food was put in front
of me, it was as if a tap opened inside my head and my tears
would spill into the rice and herbs.

During the afternoon of that first day, everyone settled
down for a siesta. Sabiha, Tanya and Ann occupied the iron
beds while Nisreen made do with a mattress on the floor, as
the room wasn't big enough to take a fourth bedstead. I had

neither bed nor mattress, so I spread some blankets in the small area of floorspace in the middle of the beds and mattress which lined the walls of the cell.

I lay down on the blankets and stared at the ceiling, considering recent events. The thought of my family and the threat of a fifteen-year sentence were uppermost in my mind. Fifteen years! No wonder Abu Samir hadn't told me what my sentence was. He knew what my reaction would have been and was probably worried that he wouldn't be able to restrain me. I had heard nothing from the British Embassy. Was it possible, I wondered, that they might intervene and persuade the Iraqis to commute my sentence? I must ask to see Robin. Meanwhile, I had to admit that there were some undeniable plus points in my new situation. I was no longer in solitary confinement, and Nisreen, the woman who had welcomed me so warmly, spoke English. Against that, Sabiha acted like a jealous lover whenever I spoke with Nisreen, demanding to know everything that was said, insisting that every question and answer be translated into Arabic.

All the effort eventually proved too much for Nisreen, who said to me apologetically, 'I must stop speaking English, Dee. I'm sorry, I have a dreadful headache. You see I haven't spoken English for five years, which, in any case, is my third language.'

Unable to restrain myself I asked another question. 'What other languages do you speak?'

'Arabic, of course, and Russian. I was given a twenty-year sentence because an Iraqi I happened to meet on a visit to Moscow told the authorities that I was engaged in espionage.'

'What about Tanya? She seems very young, why is she here?'

'Her parents are Communists, but they managed to escape from Iraq and settled in Greece. Tanya was left in the care of a relative until her family had found a new home, but when the authorities discovered what her parents had done, they brought Tanya here as a sort of hostage.'

'How long will she be here?'

'Who knows. She was brought here when she was sixteen,

four years ago. She could be here another four years or another fourteen, or she could be released in the next few days. Now I must lie down, Dee, my headache is very bad.'

I felt quite guilty for pressing the poor woman so hard, but being able to speak English again to someone was such a novelty.

'I'm sorry, Nisreen, for asking so many questions, but it is so marvellous to be able to speak English again,' I explained. 'I hope we can be friends as well as room-mates.'

She glanced over at Sabiha who lay on her bed, her black eyes glaring down at us as we chatted. 'I hope so too, Dee.'

On my sixth day in the prison a guard came to escort me to the office of the *Madeira* or Director of the prison, a woman named Senna. I later learned she had only taken up her position there seven or eight weeks previously, ousting Mohammed from his position as top dog. Senna had Caucasian features and her brown hair was shoulder-length. She wore army uniform and looked slim and athletic. She was sitting behind a polished wood desk in a large carpeted room filled with paintings, books and potted plants.

'How civilised!' I exclaimed as coffee was brought in to us on a tray, carried by a prisoner draped in a black *chador*. All the woman's top teeth were missing and I recognised her as someone I had seen through the fence between our political wing and the common-criminal wing next door.

'You're welcome,' the prisoner said in response to my '*Shukran*', which means 'Thank you'.

Good, she speaks English, I thought. The next time I saw her face through the fence I would speak to her if the guards weren't around.

'I wanted to have a word with you, Dee, before you go to the Ministry of Foreign Affairs to meet the people from your Embassy.' Senna spoke English fluently. 'I'm sorry we haven't met before, but I have been away for several days on a lecture tour. Tell me, how are you settling in?'

'As well as can be expected.' I answered hurriedly in order to get to the more important issues. 'Did you say I am to go to the Ministry of Foreign Affairs? Can you tell me when?'

'Yes, you will be going this morning at about eleven o'clock. But first I wanted to ask you if you would care to tell me something about the reasons for you being here. It is not compulsory that you do so, but it helps me if I know your background.'

Eleven o'clock couldn't be far away, I thought. How amazing, so I was to go to the Ministry of Foreign Affairs. I wondered what new twist or turn to expect this morning. I had been led up the garden path once too often to expect anything said by a prison official to be the truth, although this woman seemed genuine enough. I gave her the rundown on the trip I had made with Farzad to Hilla, and I think she believed me when I said I had not been involved in espionage and I'd no reason to believe Farzad had either. As I talked she made brief notes in a book on the desk in front of her. When I had finished the account of my 'crime', Senna closed the book and looked up at me.

'Have you got everything you need?'

Although she appeared to be sincerely concerned for my welfare, I didn't want to antagonise her and I knew that to ask for all the things I needed might do just that, so I mentioned only that I needed a proper bed to sleep on. 'At the moment I am sleeping on a blanket on the floor,' I explained.

'This I will arrange for you,' she said, standing up. It seemed our interview was at an end. 'Go now, Dee. They are waiting for you.'

Abdullah came to collect me, accompanied by a guard and a driver. When we arrived at the Ministry of Foreign Affairs, Robin and another diplomat I hadn't met before were waiting for me. We shook hands and sat down. I was happy to be having this meeting: I had wanted to see Robin, because I desperately needed to know what was happening. He would be able to tell me what had been decided. Maybe the Embassy had been able to strike some sort of deal with the Iraqi authorities. I could feel a bubbling optimism in my stomach. Perhaps there was good news – was I to be released?

Robin looked pale and strained as he leaned towards me

across the coffee table. 'Dee,' he said quietly, 'the news is not good. Farzad was executed this morning.'

I blinked at him. The whole of my body went into shock. All sense of feeling left my arms and legs so that it seemed just my whirling head was suspended in space.

'Oh, no,' I whispered. 'Oh, no, no, no . . .'

Farzad – tall, dark, handsome, funny, caring, kind Farzad. A series of pictures – edited highlights of times we had spent together – flashed across my mind. The first time I met him at the hospital when he had asked if he could telephone me. The conversations we had had about his job, the people he worked with and his ambitions to succeed in the competitive world of journalism. His hopes – similar to the ones that brought me to the Middle East originally – of acquiring furniture and hi-fi equipment for his new flat. Meals and jokes we had shared in Iraq, romantic evenings spent in London. I had never met a man like Farzad. He was tremendous fun to be with, complex, interesting, a man of many, many moods that could quickly change.

Each time I saw him I would notice something I hadn't been aware of before. We never spent a dull moment together. I couldn't believe that someone so vital could be dead.

'Did he know what was going to happen to him?' I croaked.

'He guessed,' Robin said sadly.

Suddenly I began to talk very quickly. I was aware I was gabbling, but I don't really remember what I said. My heart and my thoughts were racing along at breakneck speed. Robin put up his hand to slow me down.

'Were you there, Robin?' I asked.

'Yes. For about twenty minutes before he was taken away to be executed. The prison authorities asked me if I wanted to witness it, but I refused.' Robin raised his head. He looked terrible.

'He left you a message,' Robin said softly. 'He said, "Tell Dee I'm sorry."'

Back at the prison I fell apart. With knees jumping, hands

shaking and teeth chattering uncontrollably I sobbed the terrible news out to Nisreen, which she translated to Sabiha and the rest of the women who were crowding the doorway of our cell.

'I was all right at the time,' I sobbed, 'but now I can't stop shaking. How could they have done this? They knew he was innocent. The trial was a farce, there was no evidence against us, nothing. How can they hang a man for doing nothing?'

I was completely overwhelmed by the injustice of the whole affair. I had been at Hilla with Farzad and I knew what had happened. They knew he was innocent, I was sure of it. The trial had been a farce since his fate, and mine, had obviously been predetermined. Nothing, it seemed, could console me as my head filled up with pictures of how I imagined Farzad's last few minutes on earth must have been.

Nisreen sat by me. 'Cry, Dee. It's better that you cry here where we can comfort you. We know about the pain you are suffering. All of us have lost someone to the hangman's rope.'

From her place in the doorway an elderly woman stepped forward. She sat down beside me and took my hand. 'What Nisreen says is true. Out of forty members of my family only seven are left.'

One by one the women stepped forward to offer their condolences, translated by Nisreen. In each of their faces, the young and troubled ones and the haggard and world-weary ones, I saw a reflection of my own grief. For many of these women execution was almost commonplace; they had lost so many loved ones that way. Yet I knew they were sharing my personal pain as well as reliving their own and my heart ached, for Farzad, for them and for myself.

That night I walked the corridor whilst the others slept. From time to time shadowy figures moved in and out of the washroom. The horror of Farzad's execution stayed with me all night. I was still pacing the corridor at dawn when the other women got up to pray.

Sisters in Prison

I was tormented by images of Farzad, obsessed by what he must have suffered at the end.

The days were easier to bear than the nights. There was always plenty of noise in the prison during daylight hours and even if it was an argument in Arabic, it served to distract me from my thoughts. But every night was torture. As soon as my head touched the pillow, thoughts came flooding into my mind. If only he hadn't made the television confession. If only I hadn't had a day off. If only the car had broken down. If only I hadn't given him the empty containers. I pictured him in his blue jeans and short-sleeved shirt walking towards the gallows. What had gone through his mind? Was he aware of what was going to happen? Did they put a bag over his head? Was he drugged, numb with shock, or screaming?

By this time I was usually out of bed and pacing up and down the corridor, breathing deeply in an effort to control my accelerated heart-rate. I barely slept for more than two hours a night and usually stayed awake during siesta time. How did these women manage to sleep so much? They were in bed by midnight and although they got up for dawn prayers, they then went back to bed until 8 a.m. Only a few hours later they were asleep again, for their 2.00 to 5.30 p.m. siesta.

In the early hours of one morning shortly after the execution I lay in bed with a dozen thoughts and 'if onlys' ricocheting around my head, when I felt my arm being shaken. It was Melka, who occupied the cell next door to the washroom. She could speak no English, but was able to make herself understood as she pulled my arm.

'*Yalla*, Dee. *Yalla* (Come, Dee. Come.).'

I got out of bed and followed her to her cell, where Cheddah, her room-mate, was in the full throes of an asthmatic attack. Her face was a bluish-grey colour as she sat cross-legged on the floor gasping for air. Her fists were clenched and her shoulders hunched up almost to her ears.

I sat on the floor in front of her. Poor Cheddah, she looked quite desperate.

'*Ahney, mort* (I'm going to die),' she gasped.

'Nonsense,' I said, sounding much more in control of the situation than I felt. I took her hands and placed them, palms uppermost, on her knees, yoga-style. If only I had an inhaler, something to aid her breathing, oxygen, anything! Reaching forward I placed my hands on her hunched shoulders and gently but firmly pressed them down away from her head and into their normal position.

'Relax,' I said in English, hoping that my tone would convey the meaning. Her hands resumed their clenched position and as we went through the same routine I began to speak to her quietly.

'Just relax, Cheddah. Everything is going to be all right. Everything is OK, just relax.'

Each time I said the word 'Relax', I unclenched her fists and pressed her shoulders down. Soon all the other women in the cell were saying to her softly, 'Relax.' I sent Melka away to boil up water to create a steam-kettle in the cell. I didn't think it would do much good, but it was worth a try. It was almost an hour and a half before Cheddah's breathing improved and she lost the blue-grey pallor. She then fell exhausted on her bed and slept.

Most probably Cheddah would have recovered from her asthmatic attack without any help from me in exactly the same amount of time, but she didn't see it that way. As far as she was concerned I had saved her life, and everyone heard about it the following morning. After that I was called out regularly. There were three asthmatics in our wing and just about everybody else had something wrong with them. Iraq is a land-locked country, except for the tiny port of Umm Qasr in the south, and goitres, caused by lack of iodine, are common. Many of the women had bad backs, painful hips or knees, but without any form of equipment or access to medication there was not a great deal I could do to help them. Nevertheless, I soon found myself running a clinic from my cell, where the women would come to tell me of their ailments. I was only too happy to do this: it provided a distraction and took my mind off Farzad's death. Much of the 'medical' advice I gave them was no more than common sense and ordinary hygiene. I tried to teach them to lift correctly and to help their posture by telling them that they should carry a half-full bucket of water in each hand instead of a full bucket in only one.

I soon discovered that a nurse came to the prison between 8 a.m. and noon every day and that there was also a doctor who ran a surgery on Thursday mornings. With these facilities on hand, why would the women come to me, especially since I was so obviously ill-equipped to help them?

'Why don't the women go to the surgery?' I asked Nisreen. 'It's not difficult to control a goitre, and some of the women with a prolapsed uterus could do with minor operations.'

'They are afraid to go to the doctor because she shouts at them,' Nisreen replied.

'That's ridiculous!' I said.

By Thursday morning I had rounded up several patients, including Sabiha, who had a large goitre, and took them to the surgery. The doctor spoke English.

'Good-morning,' she greeted me pleasantly. 'What is your problem?'

'Fortunately, I don't have a problem, doctor,' I said with a smile, 'but these women have some minor ailments I think you should take a look at. You can see the goitre, doctor, I thought perhaps we could . . .'

I could hardly believe my eyes. Suddenly this well-dressed, elegant-looking doctor, who moments before had the manner of a middle-aged, Home Counties GP, was transformed.

Standing with her feet wide apart and head tilted back, she bellowed like an enraged bull at the ceiling. 'These women are political prisoners, enemies of the State, don't you understand?'

I understood that the doctor had freaked, not much else, but I stood my ground and changed tack, aware that around me my 'patients' were trembling with fright.

'Doctor,' I assumed a placatory tone. 'Please forgive me for attempting to make a diagnosis. I was wondering, out of interest, if you could confirm that this lump, for instance,' I pointed to the enlarged throat of one of my 'patients', 'really is a goitre. It's not something we see very often in England.' In fact, I had seen dozens of similar cases, but years of nursing had taught me how to handle difficult, usually male, doctors. First and foremost, bow to their superior status. This time, however, it proved ineffective.

'Of course it's a goitre. It's very common in Iraq.'

I pressed on. 'Look at this young girl, doctor,' I said, pulling a trembling Sabiha forward. 'Her lump is so large she has trouble swallowing. She is not an enemy of the State. She was too young to know about such things at the time of her arrest.'

The doctor pressed her fingers against Sabiha's throat, forcing her to gulp with fear.

'All right, she can go to the hospital, but she must pay for the transport.' The doctor turned away from us, scribbled down a brief note and handed it over to me.

'Now, go away!' she snapped.

It wasn't the best bedside manner I had ever seen, but at least one of my 'patients' was to be treated. I decided we should quit while we were ahead. We trooped back to the political wing where there was much excitement. A cup was passed around, with everybody contributing a dinar for the cost of the transport. The following day Sabiha went off to the hospital, returning with a hundred thyroid pills and instructions to take one every morning before breakfast. We watched the goitre shrink gradually over the next few weeks. I was as pleased as I might have been if I had personally performed major surgery.

The high spot of every prisoner's life was, of course, visitors' day, which assumed all the importance of Christmas, birthday and holiday rolled into one. Visitors were expected to supply prisoners' food and clothing requirements, so these visits were essential to us all. Foodstuffs were pooled, usually on a cell-to-cell basis, and even for those who had little to contribute, there was always enough to go round.

Pauline Waugh, the smiling, sensible, motherly Consul from the British Embassy was the first person to visit me after the execution. She arrived one morning bearing gifts of fresh food, fruit and vegetables – but much more importantly, the news that Michelle and Peter expected to be travelling out to see me in two weeks' time. I danced on the way back to my cell. I was going to see my daughter!

They arrived at the prison laden with gifts. It was an emotional reunion, but our conversation was closely monitored. We did not mention Farzad at all: to do so would simply have prompted the guards to bring the meeting to an immediate end. Instead, we discussed family matters such as whose dog had had puppies, where a friend would be spending a holiday – trivial issues, considering what was really on our minds.

I had been worried about the effect Farzad's execution would have had on Michelle. She was young and sensitive and I knew the Press must be hounding her for news. However, the minute I saw her I realised that she was bearing up. She looked tired and pale but she was in good spirits, and she laughed a lot as we chatted. Peter didn't say much, but clearly he was giving her a great deal of emotional support. For her part, she saw me in much improved surroundings: at least I was with other people now, and I had even made a few friends. I told her about my 'clinic' and about some of the women I had met. In spite of the circumstances and the fact that we were unable to talk freely, it was enormously therapeutic for us both.

My next visitors were Anne Morgan and Paul Coleman, colleagues from the Ibn Al Bitar hospital. I was sad to hear that several of my close friends had left – I reflected that I would probably never see them again.

At least my visits were conducted in comparative comfort. They always took place in Senna's office. Abu Samir would come over from the interrogation centre, usually with Abdullah, and take notes of everything that was said. For the Arab women, visitors' day was a much less structured affair. Each woman set off with a blanket to sit on, empty plastic carrier-bags to exchange for full bags of food and a tray of tea. When the guard came to give the word, the women rushed over to a large communal hall, each one anxious to get an area of the floorspace against the wall where she could spread out her blanket, serve tea to her visitors and chat, while using the wall as a back rest. Everyone had to shout to make themselves heard and children raced around while Mohammed and his guards patrolled the room to ensure that no secret messages or anything else were passed to prisoners. Nevertheless, it was amazing how many forbidden items found their way back to our wing.

After a visit I would be on a 'high' for several days, before dropping into a mild depression which lasted about forty-eight hours. It was usually during this 'down' period that I would ask permission to go to Senna's office, where she would take time out to talk with me over a cup of coffee.

She had lived an interesting life, working in the welfare sections of detention centres in America and Japan. 'I know how lonely you feel,' she told me. 'When I was in Japan I couldn't speak a word of Japanese and felt as isolated as you must here.'

Some time in April, after Michelle's visit, Senna told me that I would be having an additional visitor. A French journalist would be coming to the prison to interview me.

'Oh no, Senna, I don't want to see him. No, really, ask him not to come please.'

She spread her hands in a gesture of resignation, as if to say that she had no control over the matter. I went back to the political wing to talk the matter over with Nisreen.

'You have to cooperate with the authorities, Dee,' she told me.

'And if I refuse?'

'Then they will probably stop your visits.'

'So they have me over a barrel?'

'Yes, you and the rest of us. If we have no visitors then technically we could starve to death. Besides, seeing our family and friends once a fortnight helps keep us sane. It keeps us alive in every sense of the word. I am still as excited on visitors' day now as when I first came here five years ago. My mother has never missed a visit and when she goes home after seeing me, she spends the next two weeks preparing and freezing food to bring in to me on her next visit.'

Sabiha marched into the cell and led Nisreen away, leaving me with one last jealous, black-eyed, over-the-shoulder glare as they went. She couldn't bear it when we spoke together in English.

The 'French' journalist turned out to be Lebanese. He was pleasant enough. The women, their heads covered in scarves, peeped out of doorways with flirtatious eyes the day he came to see me. I must be getting old, I thought to myself, to me he looks no more than a boy.

I answered his searching questions as briefly as possible. Since the interview had been arranged by the Iraqi authorities, I knew it was not going to paint me in a good light whatever I said, so to say as little as possible was probably my best bet. However, the journalist seemed to go away well satisfied – not surprising since when I later read his article, I realised that what I hadn't told him he had made up, obviously using official documents as background.

It was genuinely funny to read what he had written. Close friends had been described as intimate friends, and whereas I had seen him as a boy, clearly he saw me as an old woman. The article made reference to many points never discussed during the interview, including a damning statement that I had discussed sending Farzad's soil samples from Hilla back to Britain via the hospital mail which, I am alleged to have told him, 'was never searched'. This, and indeed the entire interview, was complete and utter bunkum, without any foundation in truth at all, but by now that did not surprise me.

I had long since realised that truth was an eminently dispens-
able commodity where the Iraqi authorities were concerned.

I soon discovered that the humdrum nature of prison existence alters your perception of life. Possessions, for instance –
you have so few that anything you can call your own assumes
huge importance. Space was always at a premium and there
was never enough room on the cell floor for the pathetically
few items each of us owned.

Ann had moved to another cell after my talk with Senna
and I now had a bed of my own, but unless we were all in our
beds there was barely enough floorspace for the four of us
who shared the cell to stand up at the same time. Tempers
flared at the slightest provocation and everyone got in on the
act, taking sides and trying to outscream everyone else. In the
heat of the moment we behaved badly, but later, sometimes
hours, sometimes days, we did our best to diffuse our anger by
channelling it into song, mime and eventually laughter. Making a joke of bad things that happened helped put them into
their proper perspective.

After about six weeks in prison I had learned the ropes.
However, I was just as capable as the others of losing my
temper, as my new friends discovered one day when Hadi, a
middle-aged, stick-thin woman who, unusually in Iraq, had
never married, and displayed some of the self-obsessed narrow-
mindedness often associated with spinsterhood, decided
to have a clean-up. She had taken up a square of dirty old
carpet from her cell floor to hang on the washing-line and beat
it with a stick in order to remove some of the sand and dust
that seemed to permeate everything in the prison, from the
food to the beds. However, since her washing-line was already
full of wet clothes she decided, without asking, to use my little
line instead, and it broke. I was furious. It had taken me hours
of negotiation to procure a suitable piece of string to use as a
washing-line and with nothing to mend it I would be right
back where I'd started, begging for space on somebody else's
line to hang a pair of knickers here and a pair of knickers

there. Worse, to my mind, than the fact that she had broken the line, Hadi had then just picked up her carpet and taken it back to her cell without bothering to tell me what had happened. I didn't find out until I took my own bucket of washing outside and saw that there was nowhere to hang it.

'Who did it?' I demanded angrily. 'Who broke my line?'

Hadi kept quiet, but I could see the guilt in her eyes. I dangled one half of the frayed string in front of her. Nisreen stepped forward.

'Hadi is very sorry, it was an accident,' she tried to explain. I just saw red.

'Hadi, *mort* (Die)!' I shrieked in anger. The others gasped and began to whisper among themselves and shake their heads.

Nisreen, always the peacemaker, took my arm and guided me away from the group. 'That is a very bad thing to say, Dee. Hadi is upset that you want her to die.'

'Hadi's upset? Hadi's upset?' I yelled. 'So what! I'm upset too! Where am I to hang my washing? Will Hadi give me her washing-line? I don't think so. And it's not the first time she's done this sort of thing to me. Remember how she took my hot water and filled the bucket up with cold when I was out of the washroom? What makes her think she can take my hot water and break my washing-line whenever she likes?'

Nisreen looked distressed. 'Dee, you know Hadi. She is like that. She will not change, but she has her good side too. Remember how she made a dress for you when you first arrived here. Normally she charges five dinars, but she did it for you as a gift because you were so lost and lonely and because she likes you.'

It was true – when I had come into the prison feeling friendless and alone, Hadi had been one of the women who had shown me kindness. We were unable to communicate properly, but most of the women knew why I was there and Hadi clearly sympathised with my plight. I had been grateful and touched when she made me an Arab-style ankle-length dress, for it had made me feel less conspicuous than the Western-style clothing I owned. I knew, too, that she was in here through no real fault of her own. She had lived with her elderly sister until a man claiming to be a friend of their brother's, a deserter from the Iraqi Army, had arrived on their doorstep. The man said their brother needed money to escape to safety. The sisters scraped around to gather up every dinar they could, hoping to guarantee their brother's safety. However, when the so-called friend returned, he took their money and promptly arrested them – he was a member of the Iraqi secret police. The sisters were sentenced to twenty years and, for the first time in their lives, separated to serve their sentences in different wings of the prison.

Now it was my turn to feel bad, and I didn't quite know how to make amends. Since singing and play-acting were our only forms of self-expression, a song about the whole silly affair seemed to be the most appropriate form of apology.

'You're right, Nisreen. I shouldn't have said that and I didn't mean it. I'll make up a song about what happened and we'll all have a laugh together.'

'That's good,' Nisreen smiled. 'Tonight we will have a party and you can teach us the song. There is also another song for tonight about Cheddah stealing Aisha's tomato. Do you remember? Aisha was so mad that she pulled Cheddah's hair and Cheddah would not forgive her. It's very funny, you will like it.'

The party took place in the big cell where the Kurdish women lived. Tonight we were prepared to put all our differences aside. Everyone arrived on time at 8 p.m. and each guest brought something to eat and drink. The band consisted of four 'musicians', banging wooden spoons on empty dried-milk tins. We danced, we beat our chests and stamped our feet. We sang 'Cheddah ate the tomato' to the tune of 'Yes, we have no bananas'. But however much noise we made, and it was considerable, we were drowned out by the sounds of an even more raucous party taking place in the next-door wing.

'One of the women from next door is for hanging

141

tomorrow,' Alia told me, 'so they are giving her a good send-off. It's a tradition.'

Alia was around fifty years old, tall and almost scraggily built, with wrinkled brown skin and large teeth. She was something of an unknown quantity. Although she spoke English fairly well, I noticed that she only ever attempted to converse with me when there was no one else around. I never managed to discover why she was in the prison or anything about her life before she was gaoled, but she seemed to have a vast knowledge of the workings of the Iraqi political system as it operated both inside and outside the prison.

It was Alia who told me that women were hanged on Wednesdays and Saturdays, and usually given only twenty-four hours' notice of their fate. It was not always essential to have been sentenced to hang by a court: sometimes the authorities decided quite arbitrarily that the death penalty should be applied. Tuesdays and Fridays were always particularly tense days, when tempers were short and anxieties ran high: I now understood why.

'How long after their trial do prisoners wait before they hang?' I asked.

Alia shrugged. 'It depends. There's a long queue. Sometimes prisoners can wait as long as a year to be hanged, even though the hangmen work three shifts a day.'

Apparently the condemned men were not allowed any freedom of movement: they were forced to sit in a cell and await their turn for the hangman. According to Alia, there were eighteen thousand men on Death Row. 'Farzad was fortunate to jump the queue,' she said, shaking her head from side to side. 'It is a terrible place.'

We continued with our party. I performed a little song-and-dance routine about the sad demise of my washing-line, and the others joined in with the chorus.

> Hadi put her carpet
> On Dee's washing-line.
> Hadi *mort*.
> Hadi, Hadi *mort*.

We were all friends again. Next door the execution party was still in full swing when we decided to call it a day. It's difficult to imagine how someone about to die could endure such a celebration, but the following day I was repeatedly told what a wonderful last night the condemned woman had enjoyed.

I came to realise that Iraqi justice was a very slapdash affair. There was what had happened to Farzad and myself, experiences women prisoners had related of other injustices, such as children being imprisoned because of their parents' political beliefs, and then the news that prisoners could be hanged on the whim of faceless officials at only a few hours' notice. The women seemed to take it all in their stride, although frequently occasions of pleasure and excitement would be followed by periods of tangible sadness. One such example of this followed an extraordinary event in the neighbouring wing, which held the 'common' criminals, thieves, murderers and the like. Two prisoners who'd been sentenced to death on a joint murder charge were to be released, since the real murderer had been found. Relatives had arrived to collect the prisoners, bringing new clothes for them to put on, and as the women who had so narrowly escaped the hangman's noose walked towards the gate, prisoners from every wing crowded around the wire fence to say goodbye. As they walked to freedom, we waved, stamped our feet and ululated in the manner of Middle Eastern women expressing joy. It was an emotional day, offering, as it did, an element of hope for all of us. Miracles could happen, sentences could be overturned, here was the proof. Each of us followed the freed women with our eyes until they were out of the gate, praying that next time the one-in-a-million chance would be ours.

However, the atmosphere of joy was brought to an end when an almighty row brewed up between two of the women. I never did find out what it was about, but the noise was deafening as each screamed at the other simultaneously. Within minutes everybody else had joined in.

My head ached and I felt unbearably sad. I went into the exercise yard to sit beside the scrubby bush. It was known as the weeping bush and it was the only place in the prison where you could be alone. Whenever you wanted to cry, or sit quietly to sort out a problem, you could go and sit there and be sure of privacy. Everyone respected the sanctity of the weeping bush. I had used it a lot in the early days after Farzad's execution, when I felt particularly unhappy or when I was overwhelmed by the crowded conditions after my long period in solitary confinement.

How lucky the two women next door had been to be released, I thought to myself. They would be home now, doing all the ordinary things that ordinary people do. If it were me, what would be the first thing I would do? Have a long soak in a hot bath – I hadn't had a bath or a shower for almost ten months now. I often dreamed of a bath that was filled to the brim with hot, scented water, a proper lavatory, a wash-basin with soft fluffy towels hanging on a rail, a bath-room with plants and a carpet on the floor. After wallowing in the bath I would put on a long, thick towelling robe and go into my sitting-room. I would sit in every chair and then position myself by the window to watch people passing by in the street below my second-floor flat. I would watch children in uniform walking home from school, young mothers with push-chairs and carrier-bags of shopping, old women with almost empty baskets waiting for a red London bus. I would pick up the telephone and call my family and friends to say hello. I would call June, Joy, Ann, Janet and Gill. I would ring everyone I knew and say, 'Come on over, let's celebrate!'

As the weeks went by I settled down, after a fashion. Although I was now surrounded by people, my Western-ness separated me from the others and I was still lonely. I realised that the close friendship between Nisreen and Sabiha was not unusual. All the women seemed to have their own special buddy in here, someone they could confide their innermost secrets to, someone they trusted one hundred per cent. Each pair would sit close together whispering for hours on end; in fact, this was how the women spent most of their time. The relationships varied in intensity; fortunately not everyone displayed the same desperate jealousies as Sabiha, but the importance of having a special friend was paramount throughout the prison and I wished I had one too, someone I could share my jumbled thoughts with.

It is difficult to assess whether some of these intense friendships were lesbian affairs. There certainly were lesbians in the prison: generally, they were quite masculine in appearance, and some of the women would behave flirtatiously in their presence. You would often see two women in bed together, but in Iraq that didn't have the same connotations as it might in England. Particularly in the rural Iraqi villages there may often be only one bed for the entire family, which is rolled up during the day and laid down on the floor at night.

Arab women in general are more tactile towards each other, with obvious enjoyment and no embarrassment. This kind of human contact was all we had and very necessary for morale, although I think for most of us it was completely non-sexual. The women loved their buddies, but it was interesting to watch the change that came over many of them when a workman, an electrician or a plumber, was brought into the prison. They would suddenly become very feminine and seductive.

When do one's sensibilities cease to be offended? I wondered as, clutching a towel and soap, I looked around the slimy walls of the crowded washroom. Two holes in the floor served as lavatories: faeces overflowed out of them. A queue of women, many of them wearing Wellington boots, stood, seemingly unconscious of the stench, waiting to fill buckets from a tap hanging two feet above the wet, fetid floor. Somewhere in the crowd a baby was crying. A child of about three sat among the Wellingtons, poking turds with a stick.

I waited in line to fill my bucket, trying to absorb all that was going on around me. Such scenes always convinced me I had some adjusting to do. I was still suffering from a kind of culture shock.

I was not allowed to do any of the cooking for those in our

cell because I was an 'infidel', as Muslims often describe anyone who does not live by the Islamic code. In the hospital I had, of course, known many Muslims, both patients and staff, but I had never lived closely with them, as I was doing here. For the first time I realised that many compromises had been made within the hospital environment. As Nisreen explained to me, the Koran makes many allowances: for example, a pregnant woman or anyone who is seriously ill does not have to observe the sunrise-to-sunset fast during the holy month of Ramadan. But here in the prison, even if I put the kettle on, someone would get up and change the water. At first this bothered me, making me feel unclean, but after a while I didn't even notice it. It was not intended to be unkind. Muslims firmly believe in the 'rightness' of their religion and a frequently-voiced complaint is the lack of cleanliness in followers of other faiths. The devout pray five times a day, washing hands, feet and every orifice before doing so. Some Western practices, such as sharing bath-water, are regarded as horribly unhygienic.

In the cell we would eat sitting cross-legged on the floor around a dish piled high with rice and vegetables. The other women in my cell ate straight from this central dish, using – as Islamic custom dictates – only the right hand to scoop food from the dish and into their mouths. But first they would spoon one-fifth of the food on to a plastic plate and hand it to me. I was part of the group but separated by my Christianity. I learned that there had been three Christians in our wing of the prison, but under pressure from their cell-mates they had converted to Islam. Nisreen warned me I was a likely candidate for the conversion team.

'Anyone trying to force me to become a Muslim will find herself in hospital with two black eyes,' I told her. Nobody tried.

Montafa, the child I had seen playing amongst the excrement in the washroom, was a hyperactive three-year-old boy, who was compelled to destroy everything he could lay his tiny, chubby hands on. He would slip into a crowded room silently and, once inside, run amok, shouting his head off, throwing cups on the floor, or tearing up the Koran. The normally child-loving Arab women would yell at him and grab at his limbs until he was captured. A resounding slap, followed by his cries would be heard up and down the corridor at least a dozen times a day. Perhaps because I didn't slap him, Montafa developed a habit of holding on to my dress and following me around. I tried sitting him on my lap for nursery rhymes, but his concentration span was zero, so we walked up and down the yard like buddies as I tried to teach him.

> One, two, three, four, five,
> Once I caught a fish alive . . .
> Why did you let him go?
> Because he bit my finger so.

I sang the rhyme to him over and over again, but at the end of four months he was still only able to manage the first three numbers of the first line. Despite his handicap he was highly receptive to mood changes and would pat me gently if I appeared sad, clap my hands together when I was happy (usually after a visit), and respond with smiles or frowns to the tone of my voice – just as long as we were on the move. If I tried to sit down in the yard, he would dance up and down in agitation, pick up stones and throw them at cats, buildings or prisoners. Montafa's greatest joy was throwing things into the open sewers. Anything he managed to filch was tossed in with a yell of glee and a little jig of pure delight.

I became very fond of Montafa, but he was a trial. The other children in the prison were delightful and surprisingly well-adjusted. Most of them came for short periods of time, returning home to be with their fathers or other relatives after their week- or month-long visits. Salli, the small daughter of Suhad, a former television presenter who looked rather like Anna Ford, was a pleasure to have around. She spoke some English and would often sit on my bed and tell me about her brother at home and the dreadful time she had with him. Ali, a three-month-old boy, was a placid child with the same vacant expression as his mother, Hasseeba. Poor Hasseeba, she would often sit beside the scrubby bush in the yard and howl like a wolf. She had good reason. One morning a guard had come to ask her for her address, the authorities' method of letting a prisoner know that a close relative had been hanged. After an execution, Alia told me, the dead body would be taken home and the relatives would have to pay transportation expenses. If prisoners were shot, their families were required to pay for the ammunition that killed them, as well as the transportation.

In early June Michelle and Martina flew out to Baghdad to visit me. The fact that they were able to come at the same time made it a particularly enjoyable experience for me. Over the last nine months I had missed these two people more than anyone else and now we were together again. Although the girls are totally different, both are lively conversationalists with a wry sense of humour, and even Abu Samir's presence couldn't prevent us from slipping into our usual routine of teasing and retaliation. After a couple of minutes it was as if we were around the kitchen table at home.

Martina wore a pretty summery blouse and skirt and with her long naturally-blonde hair tied back in a pony tail, looked fresh and sweet. Michelle wore an extraordinary Indian type of outfit that Abu Samir greatly admired, although I did not share his taste — and what on earth had she done to her hair?

'Have you combed your hair this morning, Michelle?' I asked.

Martina rocked with laughter. 'I knew you'd say something like that, didn't I, Michelle? This is just like old times.'

The minutes flew by as we laughed and chatted together. Most of it was nonsense, but how good it felt to be able to share nonsense with them! We may have been in a stinking Iraqi prison, but it didn't stop us making the most of our time.

The humour and warmth of my daughters was intoxicating, and so infectious that at times even the frost-faced Abu Samir joined in. We went well over the hour allowed for visits before he, reluctantly it seemed, brought our meeting to an end and escorted the girls out.

I waved a smiling goodbye from the window, and watched them until they were out of sight. Then I sat down, rested my head on the coffee table and wept. Great hot tears ran slowly down my face. Where, oh where was this going to end? A hand touched my shoulder. Abu Samir was back. Waiting for the usual caustic remark I tried to swallow back the rest of my tears, but when I looked up at him I could see it wasn't necessary. His face was a study of kindness and understanding.

'I understand how you feel,' he said softly. 'I have two children of my own, younger than yours, but I do understand.'

Abu Samir's kindness did nothing to make me feel better; if anything I was even more tearful as I stammered out, 'What are their names?'

'My daughter is called Sara. She is two years old. My son, Samir, is four. I am teaching him to speak English.'

I stared in amazement. Abu Samir, the evil tormentor, the dangerous snake who had caused me so much grief over the last months, had a family. A little daughter with ribbons in her hair. A son learning English from his proud father. It seemed incredible. I had always considered that he hated me as much as I hated him. Could it be that it was just a job to Abu Samir, that he didn't hate me at all? Since I had first been arrested nine months ago, he had been the one constant person in my life. When I had left the interrogation centre I'd assumed that I had left him behind too, and I was horrified when he had turned up with my first visitors in the women's prison. Since then he had sat in on all my visits. He had heard tales of neighbours, of the arrival of new babies, ordinary things that transported me from the madness of prison and back, if only briefly, into the sanity of everyday life. Perhaps he had come to realise that I wasn't a spy at all, just an ordinary woman.

It is impossible to overestimate the importance of visiting days when you are incarcerated. Just to be able to share a conversation in fluent English rather than in my halting and inadequate Arabic was a pleasure in itself. I loved seeing my family, friends from the hospital and Pauline, who was wonderfully supportive. Her visits were popular not only with me but throughout the wing, since the fruit and vegetables she brought were always top quality.

During one of Pauline's visits I glanced up at the clock on the wall above Senna's desk to see how much time we had left.

'Where's the clock?' I asked Abu Samir, for where the clock had been a fortnight ago when Pauline was last here there was now a picture of Saddam Hussein. Abu Samir looked at me without expression. I turned to Pauline. 'I'm sure there was a clock up there the last time you visited.'

A small smile flickered across Pauline's lips and she looked down at her hands. This was when I remembered what Alia had told me. 'Whenever you see a picture of Saddam Hussein, assume that there is a listening device planted behind it.'

So, the room was bugged. Was there a camera as well? I wondered, turning my back to the picture.

On another of Pauline's visits she suggested a meeting with Michael Mansbridge, Archdeacon of the Gulf. I was against it. I didn't want to feel like 'a cause'. I didn't want men of the cloth shuttling around the Gulf (Michael lived in the United Arab Emirates) with caring smiles and worthy intentions, and I felt I knew Pauline well enough to make this clear when she suggested the meeting.

However, I found it less easy to refuse the British Ambassador, Harold (Hookey) Walker, when he made the suggestion. Hookey Walker had only recently returned from England, where he had been recalled in protest immediately after Farzad's execution. Later, the British Government decided that it was in everyone's interests, including mine, to return

him to his posting in Baghdad. I was a bit nervous about
meeting an ambassador, but Hookey Walker put me completely at my ease. As he was leaving he said, 'I'll send you in a
couple of packs of playing cards. Michael Mansbridge, the
Archdeacon of the Gulf, will bring them in to you.' What
could I say?

Michael arrived about a week after my meeting with the
Ambassador, with two packs of cards, as promised. He was
tall and rangy and filled with enthusiasm for life. We chatted
together easily for a while before he raised the subject of
Farzad. This wasn't what I wanted to talk about. Anything
but that. It was too painful, a subject pushed to the back of my
mind during the day, but which reared up with a vengeance as
soon as my head touched the pillow at night. But Michael, it
seemed, was well used to people trying to dodge issues. With a
combination of clever moves and a deep understanding of
human nature, he managed to drag my feelings of guilt to the
surface. Guilt that I was alive and Farzad was dead, guilt that I
may in some way have caused his death, guilt that my actions
in taking him to Hilla had caused his family the worst possible
kind of grief.

Then there was the other guilt, the pain and anguish I had
caused my own family, the money they were spending on
coming to Baghdad to visit me, the trouble I had caused
friends and colleagues at the Ibn Al Bitar hospital, who were
continually scratching around to find me food and toiletries in
post-war Iraq, where such items were scarce and expensive;
the guilt about the unending work I had caused the British
Embassy, who were constantly trying to liaise with the hospital, the Foreign Office in London and my family. Guilt, guilt,
guilt.

Michael quietly and efficiently took my feelings on board
before saying prayers and departing. When he had gone I
realised how wrong I had been about meeting him. He
allowed me to pour out much of what I had felt I needed to
suppress if I was to survive this ordeal. I could now see, as
Michael had suggested, that it was essential to confront my
feelings, to put them into perspective: only then would I be

able to deal with how I felt and affect an emotional 'girding of the loins' which would strengthen my resolve. I noted what Michael had said and, I believe, acted on his advice. It didn't, however, bring about a noticeable change in my personality or my temper.

A Friend of my Own

Sooner or later Sabiha and I were going to fall out. It was inevitable. One morning she sat next to Nisreen on the mattress, whispering confidences. I didn't know what she was saying, but the words 'Dee', '*Englieezi*', 'Bazoft', '*Irani*', and 'espionage' were recurring themes in her conversation today. Yet another night of pacing up and down the corridor, followed by a talking-down session to a sick and hysterical prisoner, had left me tired and irritable. I had had just about enough of Sabiha's whispered comments and the sheer gall of the woman. Even though I didn't speak Arabic, she knew damn well that I knew my own name and Farzad's when I heard them.

'What is she saying, Nisreen?' I demanded.

'Nothing much. We were discussing something in a newspaper one of the guards brought in. I don't know who has it now.'

'What does it say?'

'I don't know. I haven't seen it.'

'Well, then, ask Sabiha. She's obviously read it.'

Nisreen muttered something to Sabiha, who made a swift three- or four-word answer, shrugged and looked at me with disdain.

'Sabiha says it is better that you don't know,' Nisreen explained.

'It's not for Sabiha to decide,' I replied angrily. 'Anyway, I don't go along with this "It's better not to know" stuff. If it's about me, I want to know what has been written.'

There followed a short exchange between them during which Sabiha obviously refused point-blank to allow Nisreen to tell me what had been written in the paper. Nisreen gave me a half-shrug as if to say 'What can I do?'

'Very well, Nisreen,' I said, angry with them both by now. 'I can't force Sabiha to tell me, or you for that matter. But I would be grateful if you would tell her to stop whispering insulting comments about me. Tell her I think it's time she grew up.'

As Nisreen translated this, probably because she was too frightened of her buddy to do anything else, Sabiha's eyes began to glitter dangerously. She let forth a stream of abuse in Arabic, but I heard the word *'Englieezi'* repeated several times. She was clearly working herself into a rage. At that moment I would have liked to scratch her eyes out, but I had seen too much of that sort of thing since entering the women's prison, and had vowed I would never stoop to that level. Instead, I walked out of the building into the exercise yard. The small square of concrete was baking hot by 10 a.m., but since my blood was boiling, I thought it was probably the best place for me to be. I found a small patch of shade in a corner of the yard and practised deep-breathing exercises, reaching up to the sky with my arms, swinging them down to my toes, then up again, and down.

I sensed there was someone approaching, but I didn't stop. It was Frieda, a very large Iranian woman in her fifties. She watched what I was doing and began to do the same. Her rolls of fat wobbled as she struggled to reach for the sky, but she was a game old bird and kept it up. Fear that she would over-exert herself and collapse persuaded me to stop. I had calmed down by now anyway and realised that there was very little I could do about Sabiha: if she wanted to talk about me, let her. I sat down with my back to the wall and Frieda plopped to the ground beside me. When she had finished panting, she began to talk in a strange, bastardised form of French. Once, she explained, she had been young and beautiful and had been chosen to be the second wife of a very rich Iraqi. A son and a daughter were born to Frieda, and both wives and their children lived with the children's father on the outskirts of Baghdad.

'Didn't you mind having the first wife and her children live with you?' I asked her.

'No, it is our custom. I didn't mind.'

Apart from her special buddy, Frieda had no friends on the wing. This may have been because she was an Iranian, but it was more likely because she never stopped talking. Yap, yap, yap, she went on all day long, driving everyone around her to distraction. It was Frieda's inability to keep quiet that had landed her in prison. Seemingly, her parents and brothers and sisters still lived in Iran.

One day Frieda got a telephone call to say that her father was dying. This was during the Iran-Iraq War, so there was no question of her crossing the border into Iran legally. Frieda, therefore, made her own plans. Huge sums of money changed hands and one night she and her eighteen-year-old son set off, on donkeys, over the mountains to Iran. Led by a guide who regularly made the journey, they reached their destination without being discovered by the authorities in either Iraq or Iran.

Unfortunately, on her arrival in her home town, Frieda discovered that her father had already died. She stayed on for the funeral and set off on her return journey the following day.

All would have been well, she told me, if only she had been able to keep her mouth shut. Her husband and son were the only people who knew about the journey, and to the guide they had no names. But Frieda simply couldn't resist sharing the story of her adventure. She told a friend what she had done, the friend told a friend and the story got back to the authorities. Frieda and her teenage son were each sentenced to twenty years in prison.

As I learned the reasons behind many of the women's sentences, it began to dawn on me that Iraq was a nation of informers. No one, even in the closest of families, could really trust anyone else. This is not because the Iraqis are in any way more dishonourable than the people of other nations. What became apparent was that people were often quite simply forced to inform on friends and even family in order to stay alive themselves. If one member of a family was against the ruling regime of Saddam Hussein, and this information was not conveyed to the authorities, all the family was at risk. Mothers, fathers, brothers, sisters, cousins, aunts and uncles, as well as children and spouses, were in danger of being rounded up and either executed or given hefty prison sentences.

Some of the women were in the political wing of the prison because their husbands had deserted from the army during the Iran-Iraq War. At one point, Saddam Hussein announced an amnesty to all army deserters. If they returned to Iraq, the President said, they would not be punished. Many of them did return and, true to his word, he did not imprison them. However, the President's *largesse* did not extend to the families of deserters, so despite the fact that they returned home free men, their wives and children remained in gaol. Many of the women I knew were regularly visited by the very person responsible for their imprisonment!

'Please teach me to speak English,' implored Affra one day. How could I refuse? Affra's 'crime' against the State was nothing more than a schoolgirl's prank. As a fifteen-year-old student she had written something unsavoury about Saddam Hussein in her exercise book and passed it across the desk to another girl for a giggle. She had been spotted and the incident had been reported to the *Mukharabat*, the President's secret police. Affra was tried and sentenced to ten years.

We started off with simple words – 'blanket', 'bed', 'ceiling' – before progressing to phrases such as 'the blanket is on the bed.' Others joined in and my first English class was born. Before long I was running three classes a day. Sabiha did not approve, of course, and reported what I was doing to Mohammed. He tried to ban the classes, but was overruled by

Senna, who reckoned that anything which improved the minds of the women could do no harm.

Every morning I would do my 'rounds', checking up on the progress of people who had come to me with their ailments. Later on in the day, during the periods I had set aside for exercise, I would be joined by several other women and together we would go through an aerobics work-out. I'm sure at first some of the women thought I was completely crazy expending my energy on physical exercise, but gradually interest in my antics grew and I had an enthusiastic group. I don't know what Jane Fonda would have made of us. There wasn't a legging or a leotard to be seen: we all wore long Arab dresses, which are hardly conducive to freedom of movement. In any case, some of my group were too fat to do much more than swing their arms about in the air.

Although I thought a great deal about Farzad, I no longer suffered nightmares. Most nights I dreamed of having a friend to share my secrets with as the other women shared theirs. Sometimes she was a blonde German, at other times a dark-haired American. I think subconsciously I was trying to conjure up a buddy who bore some resemblance to Martina or Michelle. Elizabeth, when she came, looked nothing like either.

She was short and plump with a round, open face and a ready smile. Iraqi-born, she spoke four languages, including English.

'She is a Christian,' sniffed Alia, as we kneeled beside each other scrubbing at the contents of our laundry buckets.

'So am I, Alia, or had you forgotten?'

'No, that would be impossible, but you are acceptable because you are European.' Her tone implied that being European, I couldn't be expected to know any better.

'Nobody wants Elizabeth in their room, she will have to go in with the Kurds,' continued Alia. 'Did you know that she has been in the Hard Wing for several weeks?'

'What's the Hard Wing?' I enquired.

Alia dropped her voice to a whisper. 'The Hard Wing is an isolated area for political prisoners, like ourselves, except they are categorised as activists against the State. They hate President Hussein so much that his photograph had to be removed from the Wing. As you know, every public building must display a picture of the President, but they smashed the one that was there and each time a new one was brought in, they smashed that up too. Prisoners in the Hard Wing are kept locked up to prevent them from contaminating others.'

'Then why was Elizabeth allowed to come into our wing?' I asked.

'She became hysterical because the other prisoners tried to convert her to Islam. She shook the bars day and night, screaming "Jesus loves me" until eventually Senna, the *Madeira*, who is also a Christian, felt sorry for her. She overruled Mohammed and said she should come into our wing.'

Within only a few days Elizabeth and I were firm friends. We walked up and down the exercise yard for hours together. Elizabeth had married an Italian and moved from Iraq to Milan where she had two children, a daughter of six and a boy of four. One morning she'd received a telephone call from an old family friend, an Iraqi. The friend explained that he intended to travel to Italy in the near future and wondered if Elizabeth and her family could put him up for a while. She agreed.

Almost a year later, following the cease-fire agreement between Iran and Iraq, Elizabeth decided to travel back to Iraq with her children. The Iraqi secret police picked her up on arrival and despite her protests, took her and her children to the interrogation centre. Much later she discovered that during his stay in Italy her 'friend' had had connections with the Israeli Embassy in Rome. Elizabeth was charged with aiding and abetting espionage and given a ten-year sentence *in absentia* for allowing herself to have been duped. The authorities had only to wait for her return to Iraq to pick her up and implement the sentence.

Interestingly, Elizabeth and I had been in the interrogation centre at the same time.

'I heard you singing carols at Christmas,' she told me, 'and I sang along with you with the ones I knew.'

Although she wasn't tortured, Elizabeth had been knocked about quite a bit during her time at the interrogation centre. Her chief interrogator had been Abdullah, the guard from the hospital who was always pleasant to me, but whom I never quite trusted. He would, she told me, slap her face over and over again, asking: 'Why did you marry an Italian?' Slap. Slap. 'What's wrong with Iraqi men?' Slap. Slap. 'Perhaps you are too good for an Iraqi man?'

Elizabeth was smart and funny, and having her as a buddy made a huge difference to my life in the prison. At last I had someone to walk and talk with, someone who could share my hopes and fears. She was not, however, particularly popular with the other prisoners. When her daughter came to visit her, Hadi complained that her European habits disrupted the prison and Mohammed, who hated all Christians, banned the child from spending time with her mother. Poor Elizabeth was devastated, but Mohammed's word, in this case, was law.

Elizabeth was multilingual and could switch from Arabic to English to Italian without pausing for breath. After her arrest the authorities, in the shape of Abdullah, had told Elizabeth's mother that the trouble she was in was all the fault of her Italian husband, who had been implicated in the devious plot. This, of course, was patent rubbish – there had been no plot – but her mother believed Abdullah's story. After Elizabeth's arrest her husband travelled to Iraq and walked straight into a huge row, with her family accusing him of being responsible for her imprisonment. The scene ended with Elizabeth's husband and her brother having a fist fight. Her husband, outraged, returned to Italy without ever seeing his wife, leaving their two children behind. By the time her mother was allowed to visit Elizabeth and learned the truth of what had happened, it was too late. She tried desperately to contact her son-in-law to explain and apologise, but by this time he had moved away, and proved impossible to trace.

What had happened to Elizabeth, how her world had been turned completely upside-down by a simple, friendly act which had lost her children, her husband and her freedom, terrified me if I allowed myself to think about it. The way in which the authorities had tried and sentenced her in her absence and then lain in wait for her to return home to visit her ageing mother was, I now knew, typical of the underhand way the Iraqi secret police worked. How could I ever have been so naïve as to think the Iraqi people suffered from a form of national paranoia; how had I not seen what was going on in this country? Had I been so preoccupied by my own life that I had been blind to the suffering of the ordinary people I met and worked with every day?

I could only conclude that I must have been, and that I'd been too busy working and socialising to recognise all the signs. But I knew now why the Iraqis were so scared of everything and anything that smacked of officialdom. They had every right to be terrified. I know I was. It was often difficult to assess just who was the enemy. Abdullah, for example, was in the pay of the secret police and had frequently slapped Elizabeth around, but he had shown me great kindness. Senna was an intelligent and, it seemed, a compassionate woman, but how come she was running a prison? In my experience intelligence and compassion were not normally rewarded by the Iraqi authorities. At least with people like Abu Samir and Mohammed you knew where you were.

I didn't like Mohammed: all requests to him, however pressing, were treated with disdain, and his response was always negative. Although he did not personally beat up prisoners, he was not above sending female guards in to do the job for him. He was much feared by all the women. I could well imagine that the arrival of Senna, some two months earlier, had been a bitter blow to him and his professional male ego. Senna, dressed in army green, was senior in rank to him. She had put a stop to the beatings and was now engaged in getting us better sanitary arrangements. Thanks to her intervention we now received daily calls from the 'honey wagon' that pumped out the sewage.

Mohammed was incapable of displaying any such humanity towards us. On the contrary, he positively enjoyed depriving us of any comforts or privileges. One late April morning he came bursting into the wing, causing total panic as the women rushed to find a headscarf to cover themselves. Those in the washrooms without head-covers were trapped there until he left. He reminded me of Bad News as he careered up and down corridors, shouting and banging, putting his head through the doors and screaming at frightened women who were clearly doing no harm. As soon as he spotted Elizabeth he yelled at her to move her belongings into the area shared by the Kurdish women. Fortunately, Senna arrived on the wing shortly afterwards and countermanded his order.

There was a very strong division between the Iraqi women and the Kurds. The aftermath of the Gulf War focused world attention on the plight of the Kurdish people, who have suffered horribly at the hands of Saddam Hussein. However, even among the common people and before the war, I found that there was no love lost between the two. The Kurds spoke a different language, lived in their own area of the wing and were generally as separate from the Iraqi women as it was possible to be in the circumstances. The two sides would come together only to argue, even though they didn't speak the same language.

The least thing could provoke a row, but it was time spent in the washroom that led to most of the serious arguments. The washrooms were small and woefully inadequate for the number of women on the wing. Water was limited and dispensed on a strictly 'first come, first served' basis. A Kurdish woman leaving the washroom would not willingly give her place to an Iraqi, even if she was the next in the queue: she would look for a fellow Kurd to take her place. The Iraqi women took exception to this sort of treatment. Not that they weren't as bad – they looked down on the Kurds as an inferior race. I was fortunately accepted by both sides. I found the Kurdish women lively and good fun to be with, but I limited the time I spent with them, because it was so resented by my cell-mates, who clearly considered it fraternisation with the enemy.

I knew that if Mohammed had his way and Elizabeth was sent in with the Kurdish women permanently, she would become totally unacceptable to the Iraqi prisoners, so I was relieved when Senna decided she should move into a cell with Hadi, Frieda and Suhad. Hadi, however, was not pleased with the arrangement. She did not want a Christian in her cell, sharing the food in the middle of the floor. Knowing this, Elizabeth further annoyed her by insisting on eating Arab-style, taking food mouthful by mouthful from a communal dish, instead of having, as I did, a plate of her own. Hadi tried to enlist the support of Suhad, the former television presenter, but Suhad had travelled all over the world, meeting people of many cultures and religions, and didn't care who she shared her mealtimes with.

Poor Suhad was still recovering from the shock of receiving the death sentence for making a weak joke about Saddam Hussein. Seventeen days after being told she would hang, the President, in his generosity, commuted the death sentence to twenty-five years. But during those days when she feared she would die, Suhad suffered from hyperventilating attacks and lost a lot of hair through stress and anxiety.

Frieda, the Iranian, always ate alone from a tray piled high with food, so Hadi had no support for her campaign. All she could do was direct scathing remarks at Elizabeth, who usually ignored her attacks and blithely continued shovelling up from the communal dish. When Hadi became intolerable, Elizabeth would come into my cell and sit on my bed for a chat. This, in turn, would infuriate Sabiha, who would sit on her own bed and scowl at us. Using Nisreen as interpreter she told me that Elizabeth should concentrate on integrating into her own cell and not attempt to violate the sanctity of 'our family'. What a load of claptrap, I thought. Sabiha had no time for anyone but Nisreen. She didn't really feel Elizabeth was violating anything, she just couldn't bear to see us enjoying ourselves.

I resolved to take no notice of her which, predictably, made her even worse. Eventually the situation became so fraught that Senna had to intervene and organise a cell shuffle. I was to go in with Elizabeth, Frieda and Hadi, while Suhad would move into my vacated bed, sharing with Nisreen, Sabiha and Tanya. Suhad wasn't happy with this and after a couple of days came back to her old cell to eat with Hadi who, unable to face eating with two Christians, was now, like Frieda, eating alone.

The new arrangement suited me fine; it was great to be sharing with Elizabeth. What's more, we discovered that we were both insomniacs. At around midnight we would carry our blankets into the corridor and sit on the floor playing cards. She taught me a game, using two packs of cards, that we never seemed to tire of. Sometimes others would join us. They were the free thinkers, like Suhad, who were well-travelled and had once held top jobs. Together we would discuss travel, religion and men without fear of giving offence to each other. Often we would stay up until dawn, when the other women were rising for prayer. First they would put on a sort of Balaclava, which left their eyes, nose and mouth visible, then they unrolled their prayer-mats and spread them along the corridor. An embroidered cloth was spread out on top of the mat. A stone and a rosary of beads were placed at one end and facing in the direction of the holy city of Makkah, they would kneel, touching their foreheads to the ground as their lips moved in silent prayer. The ritual was repeated five times a day.

Although by this time I had been living in the Arab world for more than five years, I had never given a great deal of thought to religion. I didn't for instance, know the difference between Sunni Muslims and the more rigidly-devout Shi'ites. However, in prison I discovered that all Muslims believe in the same supreme God, Allah. Mohammed is often referred to by Muslims as God's messenger, since he is the man to whom God is said to have explained the true meaning of Islam. Mohammed is said to have recorded God's words to him in the holy Koran, for which all Muslims have the greatest respect. When Mohammed died in AD 632, he left no instructions as to who was to succeed him and there was a great deal of confusion as to who should follow in his footsteps. After several years of discussion and fighting, his followers split into two groups, the Shi'ites and the Sunnis. The majority of Iraqi Arabs are Shi'ites, although the ruling majority of the country are predominantly Sunni. There are also important minority groups living in Iraq, including Christians, Jews and Kurds.

Working in a hospital environment I had never seen any real need to differentiate between the two Muslim groups. But here in prison the differences were so apparent they could not be ignored. For example, it was the Shi'ite women who rounded everyone else up for prayer and who insisted the Koran must be read aloud, several times a day and for hours at a time. The rigidity of the Shi'ite way of thinking spilled over into every aspect of daily life. As far as they were concerned, there was only one way to wash dishes, peel potatoes or even clean your teeth, and they spared no one in their efforts to 'educate'. The Sunnis were far more easy-going, complaining incessantly about the extremism of the Shi'ites. They didn't want hours and hours of Koran reading or religious discussion, but the fervour of the Shi'ites ensured that they usually had the last word, except, of course, where the Kurds were concerned.

Seven Kurdish women occupied the large cell across the corridor from mine. All would have been well had they been left alone, for they were a jolly group, tightly knit and genuinely fond of each other. But because the cell they occupied was a large one, and space was always at a premium, the Kurds were forced to share their living area with five Iraqi women. There were constant fights, with the Arabs screaming in Arabic and the Kurds screaming in Kurdish. The Arabs did not know what the Kurds were saying any more than the Kurds knew what the Arabs were saying, but all were aware of what they were fighting for – religion, culture, order and floorspace.

'Dirty camels,' someone would sneer from the Arab side of the room.

'Tethered donkeys,' would fly back from one of the Kurds. A full-scale shouting match would very soon erupt and everyone along the corridor would spill out of their cells to watch the fun.

It was the level-headed Nisreen who usually acted as the peacemaker. She spoke some Kurdish and Curdy, one of the Kurdish prisoners, spoke a little Arabic. Nisreen would appeal to Curdy to help get things under control and would have succeeded in much less than the two or three hours it usually took for peace to resume had it not been for Sabiha, who would dart about from one group to the other doing what she could to stir things up. Sabiha loved a good row.

As far as I know all the Kurdish women, as well as the majority of the Arab women, were in prison because a relative had deserted from the army. In some cases the male relative would be captured and put into the Abu Grabe men's prison. Very occasionally, a visit to relatives in the men's prison could be arranged, and then the women would return with stories of the luxuries the men enjoyed. They had hot showers, radios and magazines and were allowed to go for long walks around the prison which, the women assured me, was as 'big as a city'. These were the plus points; on the minus side was the fact that men were housed a thousand men to a single dormitory cell. The very thought of it turned my stomach. It was bad enough sharing the confined space of a cell with three other people, let alone nine hundred and ninety-nine others.

However, there did seem to be some areas of glaring inequality. If the men were allowed hot showers, radios and magazines, why weren't we? I put the question to Senna, who agreed that it seemed unfair. I asked Pauline if she would bring me a radio, and two weeks later she duly turned up with one. I wasn't allowed to have it straightaway for some reason, and despite many enquiries, it failed to turn up. On her next visit Pauline asked about the radio, only to be told that it could not be passed on until special permission was received from the Ministry of Foreign Affairs. The following month it was special permission from a specific department at the Ministry of Foreign Affairs and the month after that it was the special permission of a certain person in a specific department at the Ministry of Foreign Affairs . . . who, that month, was off sick.

And so it went on, excuse after elaborate excuse. I never did get the radio. Fortunately, one of the other women was more successful: she managed to get a visiting relative to smuggle her a small transistor into the prison, beneath her long hair. We spent weeks in a huddle listening enthralled to 'Voice of America' and news from around the world. It was the most amazingly liberating feeling to have access to the words and thoughts of people in the 'free' world.

We were distraught when the radio had to be destroyed. Mohammed was on one of his purges, ransacking cells in the hope of finding 'contraband'. We smashed the radio up ourselves rather than give him the pleasure of doing so. He was delighted enough with his haul of dangerous and forbidden items: mirrors, marmalade pots, tiny china coffee-cups, fruit bowls and vases – he took bag-loads of them away. Poor Hadi, modest to a fault, was mortified that during his search of her cell he had seen a pair of her knickers lying under the pillow. The fact that any man, let alone the hated Mohammed, had seen her giant drawers horrified her, and she could talk of nothing else for the rest of the day.

Later, we all got together and let off steam by acting the events of the day out in crazy song-and-dance routines. Turning a bad situation into a cause for laughter diffused our anger and resentment. Without these impromptu concerts, such as the one which followed the incident when Hadi broke my washing-line, the place would have been an emotional tinderbox. I leapt about, rolling my eyes and going completely over the top. Hadi took it in good part and by the end of the evening we were all falling about laughing, the theft of our precious bits and pieces almost forgotten. By doing this we felt we had prevented Mohammed from winning. He may have stolen our belongings, but he had given us an evening's entertainment and a damn good laugh. How he would have hated doing that!

Thoughts of Escape

Heaven is an empty washroom. I crouched on the floor, lowered my head into a bucket of warm water and marvelled at the luxury of feeling the water swirling through my hair. I massaged shampoo around my scalp. Funny, I'd never realised before how sensuous an everyday thing like washing your hair could be – although this was hardly an everyday sort of hairwash. Through the tiny, open window of the washroom came the sound of chattering women. They were grouped outside around the sewers, waiting for their nearest and dearest to be frisked by the secret police before being allowed inside. It was visiting day in the political wing for everyone except me.

Suddenly there was silence. Mohammed had stepped through into the courtyard to shout each woman's name as her visitors were allowed access. 'Suhad!' he bawled out in his rough voice. 'Elizabeth! Nisreen! Asha!' I could imagine each prisoner rushing forward, covered from head to foot in her long flowing gown, hurrying anxiously toward her friend or relative, looking more like a fruit-bat in full flight than the woman they knew and, presumably, loved. One or two of them would wait in vain, clutching empty carrier-bags they'd hoped to exchange for full ones that would bulge at the seams with fresh fruit and vegetables, pre-cooked meat dishes, sanitary napkins and toilet rolls. But it wouldn't be lack of provisions that would have them fighting back the tears. Today there would be no loving embrace, no news of home, no contact with the outside world. And mingled with the disappointment there would be fear — fear that a husband, mother or brother had not put in an appearance because they had been picked up by the secret police and were perhaps even now undergoing interrogation or torture.

I sat back on my haunches and watched the soap-suds fall soundlessly to the floor as I thought back to yesterday's conversation in the 'nightclub', the name we laughingly gave to ourselves when we met up after dark for a chat.

'Cheers!' Elizabeth had said at midnight, raising her red plastic cup of coffee.

'*Marhaba!*' I replied, lifting mine. 'How wonderful it would be if a fairy godmother appeared, waved her magic wand and changed this coffee-cup into a crystal glass full of chilled white wine.'

'Served up by a beautiful blond waiter,' Elizabeth added.

'Or a dark-haired one,' I cut in.

'Any colour will do,' we chorused.

The three other women who made up the nightclub leaned forward expectantly. They couldn't understand the words, but they got the drift of our conversation and bombarded me with questions. Elizabeth translated.

'Is it true that Western women sleep with men before they marry?'

'Yes, quite often. We don't set as much store by virginity as you do in the Middle East.'

'That's incredible. An Iraqi man would not marry a girl who was not a virgin.'

I was puzzled. 'Well then,' I asked, 'what will happen to Hasseeba and others whose husbands have been executed? Will she live alone for the rest of her life?'

'No, of course not. She will become the second wife of her husband's brother, her brother-in-law.'

'Her brother-in-law! Good heavens, can she refuse?' The women saw the look of horror on my face and laughed.

'Yes, she could refuse, but it rarely happens,' Elizabeth explained. 'The alternative is to live with her parents, because an Arab woman must have male protection at all times.'

By now I knew this to be the case. Male supremacy in Iraqi society is absolute. Even in Baghdad, considered by Middle Eastern standards to be a fairly relaxed and forward-looking Arab city, it is rare to see women walking in the street unaccompanied. An Iraqi woman's role in life is supposed to be to please her man, with whatever means she has at her disposal – her body, her cooking, her housekeeping. His protection is part of the return package – and in the absence of a husband, a close male relative will be called upon to offer a similar service. In the war with Iran, Iraq lost many men, and the eldest son of the family, often no more than a child himself, had to assume the mantle of protector. The women of the household usually go along with this practice, and mothers, sisters and aunts who perhaps only ten or twelve years before had been changing the nappies of these boy-men were now dancing attendance on them.

'Supposing after she remarries she finds she doesn't like her brother-in-law, then what happens?' I asked.

'It doesn't matter whether she likes her brother-in-law or not. What is important is that she gets on with his first wife. It is with her she will share the household chores and the upbringing of the children. She will take turns at sleeping with her brother-in-law, in order to have more children, but it is her relationship with her new sister that will be most important to her happiness.'

I marvelled at the strength and resilience of the women around me. They expected so little from life and, as far as I could see, life was not disappointing them. Their acceptance of fate, be it in widowhood or imprisonment, was astonishing. It wasn't that they were complacent; it was just that they were resigned to accepting whatever hand fate had dealt them. Our language and customs were completely different, and in other circumstances we might have had nothing in common, but here we shared everything: food, laughter, tears, hopes and fears. I have never had such intimate bonds with women before.

I moved off my haunches, rinsed the shampoo out of my hair, turned on the cold tap and sat beneath it, allowing the water to splay down my back. What luxury! There was no one to bang on the door and try to hurry me out, no heated arguments over washroom space and, best of all, no let-up in the stream of water, which would usually trickle to a stop the very second I had soaped up.

My mind went back to the nightclub. After the other three women had drifted off to bed, Elizabeth and I had got down to discussing serious issues. This was what the nightclub was all about. We imagined ourselves sitting at a pavement café in Paris. A carafe of wine stood in the centre of a table loaded with cheeses, pâtés and crusty French bread. Our two companions were male, one fair and one dark.

'I shall call my man Tony,' said Elizabeth. 'What about you, what will your man be called?'

'Andrew, maybe, or Mark, or will it be Timothy? Yes, Timothy, but known to everyone as Tim.'

'Tim and Dee,' mused Elizabeth. 'Tony and Elizabeth. It sounds good, doesn't it? What shall we talk about?'

'The play we saw last night, the art gallery we visited this afternoon, the restaurant we've booked for dinner.'

'But first,' Elizabeth cut in, 'we'll drive around Paris in a car with the top down and everyone will wave to us and we'll wave back, just like your Royal Family. And then we'll go dancing. Tony and Tim will hold us close as they whisper how beautiful we look in our long dresses, gold necklaces, earrings and bracelets.' A dreamy look came into Elizabeth's eyes and I realised that she was there, in Paris, dancing the night away with a handsome man, or as close to it as she was ever going to be.

It was just a game, but it was a lifeline to us. It took us outside the grim constraining walls and transported us to places far away from the reality of life in an Iraqi gaol. We went not only to Paris but all around Europe, often to places neither of us had ever visited. When we got there we were no longer the hungry, skinny, dry-haired, broken-nailed crones we had become, but witty, vital, beautiful sophisticates. Women with tinkling laughs, who dined on champagne and caviare, and dated handsome, powerful men who drove fast sports cars through European cities.

'What sort of men do you like, Dee?' asked Elizabeth. 'Footballers?'

'Mmh, yes, I like footballers and cricketers and rugby players and . . . '

'Rugby players! But they are so big, Dee,' she giggled. 'Big shoulders, big hands, big everything, yes?'

'You sound as if you have some experience, Elizabeth.'

'No, no. I don't like rugby players. Tony will be slim with small – what do you call them?'

'Hips?'

'Yes, hips. Right, what shall we do next?'

'Let's move to dinner. We are at a wonderful restaurant where we can have anything in the world we want to eat, soufflé, tournedos, *coq au vin* . . . '

'And rice,' added Elizabeth.

'After the meal we'll invite them back to our apartment for coffee.'

Elizabeth's eyes opened wide. 'We have an apartment, Dee?'

'Yes, in Montmartre, where the artists live in studios above cobbled streets lined with flowers and hanging baskets.'

'What sort of furniture shall we have?' asked Elizabeth, warming to the idea of a flat in romantic Montmartre.

'Chairs,' I replied, straightening my back and shifting my position on the hard stone floor. 'Big squashy chairs in faded floral patterns, wall-to-wall carpeting and hot and cold water that never, ever dries up.'

Elizabeth laughed and clapped her hands together. 'And big double beds,' she interjected. 'We will live there with our men for ever and have many babies.'

'Babies! Hang on a minute, Elizabeth. I'm just beginning to enjoy the freedom of France – who wants babies? Besides, we already have children.'

We sat side by side on the stone floor and the dream dissolved as we thought about our children. I was angry with myself, wasting time on stupid games of make-believe when I should be concentrating on how to get out of this place for real. I continued to think about Michelle and Martina until the first rays of light filtered through the bars of the door and the women rose from their beds for the first prayer of the day.

I reached for a towel and wrapped it around my head before stepping into a long royal blue Arab-style dress, beaded at the neck and cuffs. It wasn't compulsory for me to dress in the same way as everyone else, but to do so made me feel less conspicuous. In temperatures of as much as a hundred degrees Fahrenheit and for sitting around on the floor, a long dress was also more practical. Arab women are modest and at no time did one even catch a glimpse of knee or thigh. I laughed aloud as I wondered how some of the women would react to our Western fashions, garments such as boob tubes and miniskirts, and made a mental note to run a census at the nightclub that night.

'Dee, are you there?' A soft voice was calling. I opened the door and looked out. It was Alia.

'Hello, Alia. Did you have visitors today?'

'Yes, it was lovely, but too short. I hear we are getting another six Kurds.'

I groaned. How did they imagine they could squeeze another six women into a prison already bulging at the seams?

'When are they coming?' I asked.

'After their trial, probably around the end of the week.'

'What?' If they hadn't yet gone to trial, it wasn't sure they would be coming here. Alia must have misunderstood.

'What do you mean, Alia, after the trial? They may not be found guilty, they may not get a prison sentence.'

'It is already decided,' she assured me. 'The Kurdish Resistance Movement have found out.'

'How do you know all this?' I asked her.

'I listen in. They speak quietly in the visitors' room, sometimes in code, but I have very good hearing.'

So, Alia also spoke Kurdish. Did anyone else on our wing know that? I thought not.

I could sense that Alia liked me, but I could never work out why she confided these snippets of information that could so easily have got her into serious trouble.

'Why do you tell me these things, Alia?'

'I trust you. If you were going to inform on me, you would have done so by now. Am I right?'

'Yes, you're right, but only up to a point. I'm not super-brave, you know. If the interrogators take me out and torture me, I shall most likely spill the beans.'

Alia looked at me quizzically. 'Spill the beans?'

'Tell everything, let the cat out of the bag, get another person into trouble with what you say. Your life could be on the line, Alia.'

She gave me a wry smile and I knew that if her life was indeed on the line, it would not be for the first time. I was filled with admiration for this brave, intelligent, multilingual woman who possessed talents that her country, still stumbling under the economic burden of almost a decade of war, so badly needed. Instead, she was languishing in prison. What an utter waste!

'You know, Alia, one of the first things I noticed when I arrived here were the dreadful scars on Bassima's arms. She was doing her laundry at the time and I couldn't help comparing her arms to a couple of slabs of cold rice pudding. Since then I've noticed it on a number of the other women. What causes it?' I asked.

'It is where they were beaten in the interrogation centre. Many of them are covered from head to toe in such scars.'

I shifted my position against the wall, horrified but enthralled.

'Have you seen the old woman with a very bad limp who's in the wing next door?' Alia asked.

I nodded. I had seen her through the wire, trying to make her way, obviously painfully, about.

'She had her hip smashed by the interrogators and is now crippled for life. Then there's Moha. You were talking to her through the wire a couple of days ago.'

'Is she the tiny woman with no teeth who serves coffee in Senna's office?'

173

'Yes, that's her. Her teeth were knocked down her throat by the interrogators. Then they hung her by her arms from a ceiling fan and switched it on so that she flew round and round. Her arms were pulled from their sockets.'

'But why?' I asked in astonishment. 'She's an old woman, what did she do to deserve that sort of treatment?'

Alia shrugged. 'She was once one of the richest women in Iraq. She owned most of Mansour, all those big houses down there and the race-track. Now she has nothing. It's all gone, you-know-who got his paws on it. They accused her of receiving stolen gold from Jordan. Maybe she did, maybe she didn't, who knows? When they need money they don't care how they get it. You and Elizabeth are probably the only women in this prison who haven't been tortured. In the interrogation centre they keep an instrument that looks like a folded umbrella, but when the end is pressed a current of electricity shoots out. They put it in our ears, up our noses and into every other orifice we've got! They even do it to virgins.'

One horror story followed hot on the heels of another. Clearly I had been fortunate to escape the interrogation centre with only a few kicks and slaps.

By now other women were arriving back from the visitors' room. Alia slipped into the lavatory and closed the door; I picked up my soap and shampoo and headed back to my cell. Just inside the door lay Sabiha, clutching her side and groaning in agony. Nisreen was kneeling beside her, stroking her brow.

'It's her kidney,' explained Nisreen. 'She has been troubled by it for many years, but it has been made much worse by the interrogators. She begged them not to beat her over the area of her kidneys, but when they knew it was a weak spot they did it all the more. Can you help her, Dee?'

I looked at Sabiha writhing in pain, and not for the first time felt the frustration of being surrounded by illness I could do nothing about. 'I wish I could help, but I have no equipment. You see there are many kinds of kidney trouble. It may be she needs antibiotics, or perhaps she should cut down on her protein, salt or fluid intake – but without diagnostic equipment such as X-rays, it's impossible for me to tell.'

We were, as the doctor had said, enemies of the State, and deserving only of the minimum of care. I knew Sabiha was not about to be whisked away for emergency treatment. It was up to me to do what I could until she could be properly treated, even though I knew I could not do much.

I emptied the last of my precious English marmalade out of its glass container and, after washing and drying the jar, gave it to Sabiha to provide a specimen of urine. I held the sample up to the light. It was cloudy and dark in colour and probably contained protein. There could have also been blood, or an invasion of bacteria present, but this was impossible to detect with the naked eye. For twenty-four hours we carefully monitored her fluid intake and urine output, using old milk cartons. There was a huge discrepancy, with her output less than a quarter of her total intake, but even this told me little, since I had no idea how much moisture was lost by breathing and sweating in the sweltering heat of an Iraqi summer. Two litres, three, maybe more – I was no further forward. I considered measuring Sabiha's liquid intake and urine output with my own, but quickly dismissed the idea. I would not represent a true guide: I was far less able to tolerate high temperatures than the others who had spent a lifetime coping with the intense heat. Often I would sit on my bed in the afternoons with sweat pouring down my face and body, marvelling at my cell-mates sleeping comfortably beneath their blankets.

Fortunately, we were able to get Sabiha an appointment to see the nurse who came to the prison every morning between 9 a.m. and noon. She returned to the cell with a number of tablets in a screw of paper. 'Kidney pills,' she said proudly, holding them aloft. I have no idea what they were or if they actually helped her complaint, but the psychological benefits of receiving them were unquestionable. From the moment she popped the first one into her mouth, Sabiha brightened up and became, if not pleasant, much less quarrelsome towards the rest of us. For several days, peace reigned in our wing.

Less than a week later the Kurds Alia had spoken of arrived in the prison. Along with them we got Muna, a twenty-two-year-old Arab woman with an unnatural grin reminiscent of the leer sometimes adopted by long-term psychiatric patients. Suhad took Muna under her wing, but this upset Hadi, who considered Suhad to be her special buddy. In order to leave no one in any doubt of her feelings she crashed around her cell, banging things about and being so disagreeable it was difficult to be around her. All that changed when Muna gave birth to baby Hassan. From her first sight of the infant Hadi was besotted with him.

Muna went into labour in the early hours of the morning, but it was 8 a.m. before she was driven to the nearest hospital by one of the many members of the Iraqi secret police who worked in the prison. At noon she reappeared in the prison courtyard, looking pale and wan, clutching a tiny bundle wrapped up as if it were bound for the North Pole. Loving hands reached out to help Muna on to her mattress. Meanwhile, Hadi unwrapped the baby, checked him over and wound him round and round in a long length of clean white cotton to prevent movement of his arms and legs which, she said, would help him grow tall and straight. Instinctively, I wanted to rush forward and unwrap the tiny mite, let some air get to his body and allow him the freedom to move his limbs at will, but since I knew that this would cause Hadi real distress, I did nothing.

Muna made a slow recovery. Her temperature shot up and she complained of aches, pains and an offensive discharge from an infection. We got her some antibiotics which helped her physical condition, but mentally she did not respond. She failed to bond with her new son, refused to feed him and was more than happy to leave his care to others. Suhad was able to obtain some tins of baby-milk powder for us to make up feeds, but in the filthy prison conditions and with so many people handling him, baby Hassan developed gastro-enteritis and became weak and sickly. Muna remained disinterested and although professionally I understood that she was suffering from a form of post-natal depression, I felt that she should at least make an attempt to put her own feelings aside and give her tiny son the love and attention he needed. Alia, however, took me to one side and explained something of Muna's situation.

'Poor girl,' began Alia. 'She's been through so much I think it must have scarred her for life.' She told me that Muna had been arrested with her husband and his two brothers for alleged political crimes. It was not until after her arrest that she discovered she was pregnant, by which time she had been separated from her husband and his brothers. Her first news of them was that her husband was dead: he had, government officials told her, been beaten to death by his brothers for getting them into trouble. Her brothers-in-law were hanged for his 'murder' and Muna was sentenced to twenty years' imprisonment.

'Of course, she does not believe the "official" version,' Alia said. 'She knows that her husband and his two brothers were tortured by the interrogators until they died. But every day she lives with the uncertainty of who killed him and why. It's hardly surprising she cannot cope with her baby and is hoping her family will take him and raise him.'

I made baby Hassan a bib out of an old pillowcase, but it disappeared. There must have been some story behind it, because the women looked embarrassed when I asked what had happened to it: perhaps they were not allowed to accept gifts from a Christian.

Baby Hassan went home with his grandmother about the same time as Salli, Suhad's young daughter, arrived for a short visit. (It was not unusual for children to come into the prison for brief visits with their mother which, considering the lengths of the sentences handed down to women by the Iraqi courts, was a good thing.) Salli was a delightful child who spoke a little English, taught to her by her father, a wealthy Iraqi businessman held in considerable awe by the secret police. Suhad's husband capitalised on this by getting extra goods past the censor, including several dozen of his wife's favourite women's magazines. A number of these contained photographs of Farzad and one even had a picture of me on the front cover but, try as I might, I was never able to get to know the full story that was printed inside the magazine. It was, I was told by the women I asked to translate for me, just a lot of propaganda that I would find distressing to hear.

Salli celebrated her seventh birthday, an important coming of age in the Muslim religion, in prison while spending two weeks with her mother. For the event, Hadi made her a pretty white dress and a sort of Balaclava, which Iraqi women use for prayer. As the sun went down Sabiha, who was in charge of prayer calls, banged on the iron bars of the door with a stone to summon the women. I was outside in the courtyard, walking aimlessly up and down, when Salli came running out, looking like a snow princess. Her dark eyes danced with excitement as she spread out her prayer-mat for the first time and copied her mother's movements, standing, kneeling, kissing the ground and moving her lips in prayer. When she saw me watching her a big grin spread across her face. Her expression took me back years, to when Michelle was in her first school play.

Then, to the consternation of the kneeling, praying women, Elizabeth came out into the courtyard and, turning to the west, the opposite direction to the holy Islamic city of Makkah in Saudi Arabia and the direction towards which all Muslims turn to pray, put her hands together to pray to Jesus. Elizabeth was clearly aware of what she was doing and although I could understand her actions – life was not made easy for us Christians in a predominantly Muslim prison – I felt she was being rather silly. I could sense the fury that was brewing up among the women at prayer and wanted no part of it. It seemed to me we had enough to contend with in here without religious antagonism, so I returned to my cell and lay down on my bed.

There was a tap on the door and I looked up to see Anisa, a tall, dark-skinned woman of around forty, of Saudi Arabian descent. Anisa spoke some English which, together with my rapidly-improving Arabic, enabled us to have a conversation of sorts.

'Come in, Anisa,' I said. 'How is it you are not at prayer?'

'I have – what you call,' she tapped her stomach, 'unclean. We are not allowed to pray at such times.'

'Why?' I asked. 'Doesn't Allah love you when you have your period?' Anisa looked offended.

'It is our custom,' she said and then, as if in retaliation: 'You, Dee, never pray at all.'

'What do you think I should pray for, Anisa? Water? Death to the secret police? A decent night's sleep?'

'You should pray for your release, to be reunited with your family.'

'I don't think that would work, Anisa, do you? If prayer could get us out of here I would be the only one left.'

Anisa immediately saw the funny side of my argument and we laughed together.

'Why are you standing in the doorway, Anisa? Come in.'

'No, your room-mates would not like.'

'I live here too, and I'm inviting you in.'

'Well, just for a few minutes,' she said with a smile. She slipped off her shoes, as is the Arab custom before entering the home of another. As she did so, I saw her scarred toes, where her nails had been pulled out in the torture room. She padded in, barefoot, and sat down on my bed. Earlier I had been working on making a bag for Tanya's birthday, which was not far away. With a rough needle made from wire taken from the perimeter fence and an agricultural bag which had once contained cattle-fodder, I was trying to create a stylish accessory to mark the event. The bag had three pockets, on each of which I had embroidered the name of the home town of one of my former cell-mates: Baghdad for Nisreen, Rasdiya for Sabiha and London for me. Above each town I had fashioned a symbol: a sun for Nisreen, a moon for Sabiha and a star for me.

Anisa picked up the bag and began to examine it. Suddenly a look of horror crossed her face. 'Dee,' she hissed, 'you have made the Star of David!'

I took a closer look. What was the woman talking about? As far as I was concerned a star is a star is a star.

Anisa dropped the bag like a hot potato and hurried from

the room just as the women were rolling up their mats and removing their Balaclavas. The news of 'Dee's Star of David' spread like wildfire through the prison and next morning, Senna came to my cell in the hope of sorting things out.

The other women were asked to leave and to close the door behind them.

'Now Dee, what is all the trouble about? May I see the bag?'

I pulled it out from under my mattress and thrust it at her. She carefully counted the points of the star I had embroidered. She looked up and smiled.

'No problem. The Star of David has six points, yours has only five. I will let the other women know and put an end to all this nonsense.' She went out of the cell, leaving me alone. Release of the fear and tension that had been building up inside me since Anisa hurried from my cell the previous evening left me angry. I ripped out the embroidered sun and moon and star and threw the wretched bag under the bed, hoping never to set eyes on it again.

The following day I received a letter from a stranger. A British journalist living in Germany. 'As I look up at the gleaming stars on my solitary walls,' he wrote, 'I bounce my thoughts to you in far-off Iraq.'

I went outside and looked up at the sky. Stars, which yesterday had caused such a rumpus among my friends and cell-mates, were today a sign of friendship. Someone had cared enough to write and the censor had allowed me to receive it. I was filled with loving thoughts for this stranger and bounced them back to him in distant Germany – although whether he got them, I guess I'll never know.

A few days later Senna came into our room and said she had something to tell us. She was going to Germany for a month, but everything would continue as before. We shook hands and I could see something unfathomable in her eyes. She's not coming back, I thought – God help us.

No sooner had she left than Mohammed came on a purge.

He took my precious playing cards and a huge pile of goods that Senna had allowed, as well as many forbidden items. Anger rose up inside me as I imagined him taking my cards home and using them to entertain his friends. I didn't challenge him on this but attacked him on the subject of our lack of water instead.

'There's not a drop of water in our wing. Nothing is coming out of the tap and we have used up all our stores. The temperature is somewhere in the region of fifty degrees centigrade! At best we shall become dehydrated, at worst we'll die of thirst.'

'*Shweya, shweya*,' Mohammed said, which was his stock reply and meant that nothing would be done. When he had gone for his siesta, I slipped across the courtyard carrying two empty buckets. We might not have water, but I knew from previous occasions that the barrel feeding the guard's quarters would be full. I smiled sweetly at the secret policeman on duty and he turned away as I filled my buckets and carried them back. It didn't go far: by the time the children had taken their fill there was only a cupful each. I went back again, but Mohammed must have woken up, because I was turned away. By night-time all of us were parched, and we lined up at the washroom tap with empty buckets and plastic bottles. The Arab women were down on their knees praying for water, but none came through.

'*Macko Moi* (No water),' said Hadi, beating a rhythm on her chest.

'Yes, *Macko Moi!*' I joined in, keeping up with her rhythm. Others did the same, and I led a group out of the washroom into the courtyard chanting our slogan. '*Macko Moi! Macko Moi! Macko Moi!*' The women covered their faces and kept well behind me, ready to run if Mohammed came out to punish us. The thieves and murderers next door joined in the fun, and soon the entire prison was yelling for water.

Mohammed must have gone home and been recalled by a secret policeman who didn't know how to handle the situation, for after what seemed like hours of chanting we saw the lights of a car and all of a sudden there he was, striding

towards us from the other side of the courtyard. The screaming stopped as if by magic and we all ran like rabbits to the
sanctuary of our cells. An hour later, water flowed through
the tap.

Afterwards, when Nisreen and I were alone in the washroom, she turned to me with a sweet smile and said, 'You
know, Dee, I was thinking, you have a fifteen-year sentence
and I have twenty years but, since I have already served five
years of my sentence, we shall be released at the same time,
maybe even on the same day.'

I know she was only trying to be nice – Nisreen would never
knowingly hurt anyone – but her words cut me to the quick. I
looked around. Fifteen years of this pigsty of a washroom, the
overflowing drains, the flies, the filth, fighting over water,
washing-lines, floorspace. No thank you, I thought, better a
bullet in the back. And, as the thought crossed my mind, I
realised it was true. I couldn't allow myself to be resigned to
remaining in this prison for fifteen years; I would get out or
die in the attempt. I began to plan my escape.

Escape, danger, freedom, the words burned a hole in my
brain. I went out into the exercise yard and looked at the
singly-dry, spindly tree that grew up alongside the prison
wall. It was a poor specimen, a sorry apology for a tree really,
but I thought it might take my weight. I could be no more than
fifty kilos and probably nearer forty-five. If I could shin up the
tree, that would take me right to the top of the wall. On top of
the wall there were two strands of wire which, I thought,
would be easy enough to step over, then there was a drop of
about fifteen feet on the other side. I could handle that; I was
fit and light.

But it would be foolish to attempt it in daylight. The yard
was in full view of the women, the guards and the secret police
who occupied offices in the prison. Unfortunately, we were
locked in our wing at night. We could get up and leave the cell,
wander around the corridor, or visit the washroom, but we
couldn't leave the building. At dusk a guard locked us in for
the night from the inside. After socialising with us for a couple
of hours she hung her clothes up on a nail behind the door of

Hadi's cell and settled down to sleep on the cell floor. I had heard her snoring on many occasions, when I had spent the early hours pacing up and down the corridor. And judging from the general cacophony of snorts and wheezes that usually emanated from her cell, neither Hadi nor the others were troubled by insomnia.

I decided that it would be comparatively easy for me to take the keys from the guard's coat pocket as it hung behind the door while she slept. Then, in the wee, small hours of the morning, I would let myself quietly out of the building. In my mind I went over every escape story I had ever heard or read about. Escaping prisoners would often go through water, so that if dogs were brought in to track them down, they would lose the scent. Also, it was usual for them to try to disguise themselves to resemble the enemy. They saved up food and water to use on the journey, and they liked to have a safe house to head for. Where would I find a safe house? I couldn't incriminate anyone else. But of course! Three friends of mine rented a house near the Babylon Hotel. It had a flat roof with a wall around it, which they used as a patio. If I could climb the wall from the outside, perhaps I could hide out there. But no, I realised that wasn't a good idea. It was probably impossible to climb the wall from the outside, but even if I managed it, the authorities would expect me to head north in to town, towards the safety of the British Embassy or the hospital. I would be a sitting duck, and God knows what might happen to anyone trying to shield me.

Mentally, I went over the geography of Iraq's borders. Over to the west was Jordan, then, in a clockwise direction, came Syria and Turkey. Iran was to the east, while Kuwait and Saudi Arabia lay to the south. I immediately dismissed the neighbouring Gulf states of Kuwait and Saudi Arabia: they had been very supportive of Saddam Hussein during the war with Iran, supplying arms and money to arrest the spread of Khomeini-style Islamic fundamentalism. To be picked up in either one of those countries would probably result in my being sent back in handcuffs to face an additional fifteen years for attempting to escape. Jordan, Turkey and Syria were all possibilities, but I knew Iran was my best bet. The Iranians would be only too happy to help me if it involved adding to the Iraqi embarrassment at my escape. I was sure I had heard that there was still either a Swiss or a Swedish Embassy in Tehran, handling the affairs of European nationals in the country. That's where I would head for. If Frieda could travel over the mountains on a donkey then so could I! In the past I had ridden donkeys, horses, ponies, camels; no problem there. Then I remembered that Frieda had her son for protection. Well, I would just have to stand up for myself. I would be able to do it, unless, of course, an attacker had a gun. I would have to be prepared for that. Better to be raped than shot, but, if I was well prepared, I could avoid both. I could intensify the aerobics.

I was already taking two classes; I would increase that to three and make sure that as well as instructing I was also getting three really good work-outs every day, so that I became super-fit.

I thought of the desert trips I had taken to the west of the prison. If I could get to the lakes, an area I knew as well as any in Iraq, I could swim across to the other side. The chances were that somewhere along the journey I would come across a herd of camels. I had been told that unlike horses, camels do not attempt to run away from humans. If I could make a sort of bridle in advance, preferably before leaving the prison, I could pop it over the head of one of them and mount it. Would the whole herd trail along behind us? If so, the owner of the herd would be in hot pursuit. That could be dangerous. What I needed was the maximum possible time to get away from the lakes and head north-east to the mountainous region between Iraq and Iran. I knew the trip would be difficult, but I was used to roughing it, having walked the Pennine Way a few years earlier. I recalled the trip, where every step of the route along the spine of England was into deep mud or soft peat. The rain had come down in torrents for several days. Surely it couldn't be that bad. Well, even if it was, I would cope.

First and foremost, I would need supplies. I would start saving provisions, and I would ask Pauline to bring in a ball of string; I'd tell her I wanted to make a new washing-line, and then use it to make a camel bridle. I thought back to the horses we used to keep – Golden Shadow, Spotty, Comice. How often I had cleaned their bridles, especially before Michelle was due to ride them at a show! I knew exactly how to make one, but it would have to be padded if it were not to cut into the camel's face. Wool would be needed and I would have to make the bridle in secret, behind the closed door of the washroom during siesta time. Not even Elizabeth must know what I was up to, or it would put her in danger.

Then there was the disguise. When I'd first entered the prison the women, who were all dark, had showed an infuriating preoccupation with my blonde hair. They wanted to sit and stroke it – it drove me mad. I had mentioned this to Senna and she had given me some dark hair dye. I had never used it, partly because the women had quickly lost their fascination and also because I'd thought, without really knowing why, that one day it might come in useful. If I got Elizabeth to crop my hair and then dyed it black, I felt sure I would be able to pass for a small, wiry man. I had never been thinner – I had almost no bust left to speak of. Everything was falling into place.

I would need to spend a lot of time on planning if my scheme was to have a chance of success. But time was something I had plenty of. However meticulous my plans, they were not going to take me fifteen years to complete.

On my Way

The end, when it came, was swift and unceremonious. I was talking to Elizabeth in the queue for the washroom, when a female guard came tearing across the concrete yard, spotted me in the doorway and exclaimed, 'Dee, you release!'

I was stunned by her words. I made no comment at all, simply stared at her.

'You release, you release,' she babbled, while closing together her fingers and thumb to make the sign of an aeroplane taking off, like a child at play.

The women, chattering excitedly, gathered around the door.

'*Yalla!*' said the guard, plucking at my sleeve.

'No, no!' I tried to shrug her off, fearful of losing my place in the queue. 'I must wash.'

'No wash. *Yalla!*' she yelled into my astonished face.

I grabbed Elizabeth by the hand.

'Come with me, Elizabeth. It might be a trick.'

'No, Elizabeth not come,' said the guard.

'Yes, Elizabeth come.' I spoke in pidgin English, terrified that something awful was going to happen. Michelle had visited me only a few days earlier: had our conversations caused offence? I dragged Elizabeth along behind me, ignoring her pleas.

'Let me go, Dee! Mohammed will be angry with me if I go with you. Please let me go,' she begged.

But I hung on, hauling her across the concrete, through the archway and along the path to the office where I had first been given the news of my fifteen-year sentence. The same three men were sitting behind the same long wooden table, still arranged like an office desk.

'What's happening?' I asked them. Elizabeth translated. One of the men examined a sheet of paper and spoke rapidly to Elizabeth.

She looked at me. 'He says you're to be released.'

It seemed to me I had been here before. 'May I see my release papers?' I enquired.

'There are no papers.'

'But there must be. No one can be released without papers. Have they not been sent over here yet?'

'You do not need papers. They are unnecessary.'

'Come with me,' one of the other guards instructed.

We followed him into what had been Senna's office. How I wished she were here now! She was the only Iraqi official I could trust. Senna would have told me the truth, however unpalatable. Inside the office four men I hadn't seen before were waiting. One of them at least spoke perfect English.

'Why are you wearing Arab clothes?' he asked.

I didn't answer him. I was confused. Of course I was wearing Arab clothes, I was in an Arab prison. What did he think I would be wearing, a miniskirt?

'We must move quickly. We are taking you to the airport.'

I looked at the four heavies assembled in the office and felt a sharp stab of fear. It was Tuesday – tomorrow was one of the two hanging days for women.

'I don't need four men to take me to the airport, just a driver. In fact, I would rather go to the airport by taxi, if that's where I'm really going.'

'Of course you are going to the airport. You are going to your home.' His words cut into me as efficiently as any knife. Home, home, was I really going home? I wanted to believe him, but I knew it was a fifty-fifty chance: either he was lying, or he was telling the truth. I suddenly thought about my passport. If I was going home, I would need my passport.

'Where is my passport? I will need my passport,' I insisted.

He reached into his pocket and produced it. I flicked

through it quickly and looked up at him.

'There is no exit visa in here. No one can leave Iraq without an exit visa. Where are you taking me?'

'To the airport,' he replied, stony-faced.

'How can I leave Iraq without release papers from the prison, or an exit visa in my passport, to allow me to get out of the country? It's impossible.'

We stared at each other suspiciously.

'Where are you from?' I asked pugnaciously. 'Are you from Abu Grabe prison? I haven't seen any of you before.'

'I am from the Ministry of Foreign Affairs. I am a translator.' I felt a sudden lurch of fear in the pit of my stomach. Of course, that's what was wrong.

'Why have they sent you? Abu Samir is a translator, my translator, why isn't he here?'

'He is away on a course.'

'How strange,' I said. 'A few days ago I was told he was off work sick. Now you say he is on a course. What has really happened to him?'

'Nothing has happened to him. He is well. Come now, we are late. We should have been out of here an hour ago. The flight should be taking off in five minutes' time.'

'And I suppose you are going to tell me that a scheduled flight to London will sit on the Tarmac and wait for me to arrive, are you? I am not royalty, you know, and I'm not stupid either.'

'We know that.'

'I must speak to someone from the British Embassy.' I thought it and spoke it simultaneously. 'I'm not going anywhere until I've spoken to Robin or Pauline.'

That was it, I had made up my mind. I sat down and looked at Elizabeth. She was very pale. I noticed tiny beads of sweat on her upper lip and fear in her eyes.

'It's Tuesday,' I whispered.

She nodded, without speaking. So the thought that I might be taken off to be hanged had occurred to her too.

My mind was racing now as the four men talked among themselves in Arabic. Why was he holding my passport? Was it to hand to Robin after my execution? Robin had been asked to wait until after Farzad had been hanged. Was he then handed Farzad's British passport to be sent back to London in the diplomatic bag, while Farzad followed in a wooden box?

The translator moved to the telephone and put through a call. He hung up and waited for someone to ring back, then handed the telephone receiver to me.

'Hello,' I said guardedly.

'Congratulations, Dee!' said a male voice. It wasn't Robin.

'To whom am I speaking, please?' I enquired coldly.

'It's Hookey, Hookey Walker. We're all at the airport waiting for you.'

Now I recognised the voice. It was the British Ambassador's.

'Thank God for that.'

'You're being flown to Zambia.'

'Zambia? Why Zambia?'

'Don't look a gift horse in the mouth, Dee.'

'I'm on my way.'

Elizabeth and I raced back to the wing. She had spoken to the driver and was now convinced.

'I talked to him when you were on the telephone. He told me he has instructions to take you to the airport. By the blood of Jesus, it is true!' She threw her head back and laughed.

I still had reservations. It had all happened so quickly – by rights I should just about be getting to the head of the queue for the washroom. Suddenly, I was agitated, confused, panic-stricken.

'Write to me, Elizabeth! You've got my address. Write to me as soon as you are released, promise?'

'I promise!' We hugged each other, both of us crying.

I ripped off my long Arab dress and pulled on a pair of jeans and a blouse.

The women forgot the normal courtesy of standing in the doorway waiting to be invited into the cell. They crowded around me, talking and laughing. In danger of being crushed by the throng, I was unable to grab more than a few things to stuff into a plastic bag. Sadly, I could not get to the bed to retrieve all the letters of support I had received from friends and well-wishers, letters that had kept me going over the months, letters I promised myself I would answer as soon as I was free. They were left in a cardboard box under my bed with my growing escape provisions – my most treasured items.

I forced my way through the crowd of women, kissing faces and squeezing arms as I fought to get out of the door. Alia grabbed me and pulled me close. 'Tell everything,' she hissed.

I ran across the concrete yard for the last time, even turned back. The women stood shoulder to shoulder, no longer looking like a flock of black crows in their long black Arab dresses, but looking now like my friends. Some had fallen to their knees in prayer, others were waving and ululating loudly.

'Goodbye Dee, goodbye Dee . . . goodbye!'

I gave them one last wide wave and ducked into the back seat of the Ministry car. Two of the four men who had been waiting for me climbed in on either side of me and the car swept through the prison gates and headed north. Well, this was it – we were either on our way to the airport or the hangman – I still wasn't absolutely convinced. A shiver of fear ran through me when instead of turning off west towards Saddam International Airport, we continued northwards towards Abu Grabe prison. My mind went into overdrive. It was a trick. It hadn't been Hookey Walker on the telephone – that's why the interpreter had waited for someone to call him back. I had been conned, stitched up. Oh, but they were so clever at deceiving us! I remembered the previous occasion when I'd been told I was going to the British Embassy and I had ended up in the women's prison. I remembered how Abu Samir had laughed as he'd told Farzad, 'No, the judge said he was not going to hang you.' No doubt they'd smiled at Farzad, too, as they'd slipped the noose around his neck.

The car stopped in town and one of the men got out and disappeared from view. I knew by the sick feeling that was washing over me that my blood pressure was dropping. My heart was hammering against my ribs and my palms were wet with sweat. The translator returned to the car and handed me a bunch of flowers. My God, what was going on? I wiped my dripping hands on my jeans and took the flowers. The car carried on towards the race-track, then the flag-poles in front of the Trade Fair Building came into view. We entered the gates and drew up in front of the reception area. My mind was in a whirl. Why were we at the Trade Fair Building? Was I dreaming this? The airport was far away to the south-west of the city. I must be dreaming, this was a nightmare. Dear God, please let me wake up now! I will never, ever complain again about lack of water, faeces on the floor, overcrowding, jealous buddies – just let me wake up!

The car stopped and I was ushered into the reception area. Hookey Walker stepped forward to greet me. I can't remember whether we shook hands or whether I fell into his arms and wept. Pauline, dear Pauline, was there too, with a big hug and some words of advice. I went through the motions of a press conference, but I remember little except the flashing lights of a dozen cameras before it was time to say goodbye.

As we stepped out into the sunshine from a rear exit, I saw a beautiful little blue-and-white jet aircraft standing on the Tarmac. Was this for me? Wake up, Dee, for Heaven's sake! I climbed aboard, accompanied by the translator and one other person from the Ministry. I couldn't help thinking how much Abu Samir would have loved this job, jetting off to foreign parts to use his translating skills. I looked through the aircraft window and waved to Pauline and the Ambassador as we taxied down the runway for take-off.

Iraq fell away to port as we climbed into the blue sky. I looked down. Somewhere down there was the hospital I had worked in, doctors and nurses I had worked with and laughed with, hotels I had dined in, bars I had drunk in. The Rashid Hotel, with its wonderful swimming-pool, the Melia, where I had first had dinner with Farzad. Somewhere down there was a part of the person I had been but no longer was. That part of me I left in a concrete cell in a prison full of innocent victims, many of whom were my friends. I was one of the lucky few: I was going home.

Living for Today

The telephone rang a couple of times at about nine o'clock, but I'd set the answerphone so I didn't bother to get up. I was dead tired, having lain awake for hours the previous night thinking about my last visit to Mummy. There had been something very different about the way it had been conducted, and that worried me. For the first time ever we had been able to talk alone, without the presence of Abu Samir or any other Iraqi official. No doubt the listening device had remained in place, but away from the restricting presence of a third party we had spoken together far more freely than I now considered wise. Not only did we feel able to talk about Farzad for the first time, but Mummy recounted horrible stories of the torture and abuse that one of the women in her wing had told her took place in the prison.

I was half-asleep and having some kind of dream when, through the haze of exhaustion, I heard a man's voice leaving a message on the machine. It was David Hope, a Foreign Office official with whom I had been in regular contact. I should have jumped out of bed and picked up the receiver but his message immobilised me. 'Michelle, please call back, it's urgent!' I froze. It could only be bad news. They were going to hang Mummy. My mind flew back again to the unguarded conversation we had had just four days ago in the prison. Of course, of course, it had all been a trick, a plot to incriminate her further and now, because of her conversation, they were going to execute her. How on earth could we have allowed ourselves to be taken in yet again.

I tried to calm down but it was useless. It never entered my head that the purpose of David Hope's telephone call was to relay good news, and the certainty that I was going to hear something devastating prevented me from returning his call. I just couldn't get up. I lay in bed and pulled the covers up to my chin: I needed five minutes to

192

pull myself together for this news. I watched the minutes flick over on the digital clock by the bed – five, ten, fifteen – I still couldn't do it. When the phone rang again twenty-three minutes later I nearly broke my neck getting to it, but even then I was so desperate to prevent David giving me the bad news that I prevented him from getting a word in edgeways. I talked incessantly – about my tiredness, the eighteen-hour stopover at Cairo airport I'd had on my return journey from Baghdad, everything and anything to stave off the moment when he told me Mummy was dead.

Finally David managed to stop the flow. 'Michelle! Michelle, listen to me!' he said. 'She's been released! She's on her way to the airport right now! Don't say anything to anybody yet – we don't want the Press to know until she's left Baghdad. We'll release the information as soon as her flight takes off.'

I replaced the receiver quietly and felt an enormous grin spread across my face. She was free. Immediately the phone rang again – a news agency wanting a comment. So, the news had been released: Mummy's plane had left Baghdad. I didn't whoop with joy or even cry. All I could register was that she was out, and she was coming home. I telephoned all the friends and family I was able to reach with the news and within minutes the flat was besieged by journalists wanting statements, comments, interviews. Lots of them had become friends over the months, and as well as getting a story they wanted to share in the celebrations. I asked them to give me half an hour to prepare some sort of statement, and when I eventually let them in many of them bore flowers and champagne. By this time, however, the full impact of the news had sunk in, and I reminded myself that although this was a wonderful day for us, it would be especially hard for Farzad's family and friends, many of whom I had met in the course of campaigning. Farzad would not be coming home and their grief, I knew, would be acute, since our good news could only remind them again of their loss.

I was told Mummy would be arriving at Gatwick airport early the following morning after spending a night in Zambia. For me, this time was spent with the Foreign Office and giving press interviews. Many people had offered constant support throughout the months my mother was held in Iraq and I was anxious to let them know how much I appreciated their efforts on our behalf.

I would like to be able to say that my reunion with my mother was idyllic. If I did, it would not be true. I wanted to meet her on the Tarmac at Gatwick airport, but I was late and when I arrived there she was getting ready for a press conference.

I remember feeling very protective of her as she faced the microphones and answered the questions fired at her from all sides of the room. She was calm and unruffled and, I thought, gave a very good account of herself. After the press conference we were driven away to the Sussex hotel where we were to spend the next two weeks. By 9 a.m. we were enjoying a champagne celebration with friends and family but to me it still felt like a dream. Only occasionally did the thought that this was it, this was the day we had all been working towards, come into my mind.

Over the course of the next two weeks my relationship with my mother was strained and difficult. Once the welcome-home party was over I felt deflated. I couldn't really come to terms with my mother: it was as if I had built her up to be something almost superhuman, but she was just the same as she always had been. I know I was impatient with her. I wanted her to be able to wipe what had happened right out of her mind. I wanted her to forget it all, preferably immediately, so we could begin to enjoy ourselves again. In order to bring this about I tried to talk about Farzad straight-away, to get it out in the open so that it wouldn't suddenly hit her weeks later. I was desperate to get her back into normal mode, using ways I now realise were clumsy and inept. Naturally enough she set up a sort of barrier, but at the time I wasn't able to understand what was going on. It seemed to me that she resented me and my efforts and I was in tears quite a few times.

It was during the holiday in Zambia, when we were alone together for three weeks, that we began to pick up the threads of our relationship. Both of us were facing a period of readjustment. For Mummy, it was coming to terms with life after Iraq and learning to face the guilt she felt at being alive when Farzad was dead, at being free when so many of the women who had become her friends continued to suffer under the jackboot of Iraqi oppression. For me, it was adjusting to life out of the spotlight. My main objective had always been my mother's release, but I cannot deny that there were aspects of my 'celebrity status' I had come to enjoy, such as being taken to television studios in chauffeur-driven cars and asked to comment on various topical issues in the company of politicians and government ministers. Campaigning for Mummy's release had been the pivot around which my life revolved. Now she was free I didn't really have anything to do any more: I was just treading water, and I wasn't sure in which direction I should be moving.

I would also have to adjust to life as an unattached woman. Pete and I had decided to call off our wedding plans. Over the months my mother had been in prison he had been a wonderful source of support, even when I behaved far from rationally, often screaming at him that he did not understand how I felt. How could he? Even I didn't know what was going on inside me most of the time. I needed to be brought back down to earth, and exchanging thoughts and ideas with Mummy in Zambia, which was neutral territory for us both, helped that process. When we returned to London we were no longer strangers, but mother and daughter once more. We decided that we would share the London flat again, which we continue to do.

People still ask if the experience of what happened to Mummy changed me in any way. I know it changed me completely. The whole thing was a terrible tragedy that should never have happened, and although I will never forget some of the horrible gut-wrenching feelings and would never want to go through them again, I know I am a better person for having lived through the experience. Those months when I was campaigning made me aware of things I had never before considered. I think I used to be quite a trivial person – now I am much more aware of what is going on around me. Inasmuch as I ever considered the law, I used to be in favour of capital punishment, but now I am fervently against it, because I have realised that innocent people can be caught up in situations not of their own making. Before I only saw things in black and white; now I can recognise the various shades of grey in between.

I have become involved with various organisations that campaign for prisoners abroad and I hope to continue with this. I would also like to see some special counselling body set up to help people such as myself when close relatives are taken by foreign governments. The British Foreign Office gave me a contact number I could use at any time and I frequently did use it, once in the early hours of the morning when my mother's situation seemed particularly hopeless. But an independent body, with no 'official' government status would, I believe, be invaluable to relatives in the same situation.

I knew nothing about the Middle East region before my mother's arrest, but I now follow developments in the area avidly and plan to visit a number of countries – including Iraq – in the future. I would like to see Jordan, Syria and Egypt. I do enjoy the company of Middle Eastern people, and when travelling on an Arab airline to New York recently I remembered just how much I admired the warmth and generosity of the Arabs.

I recently started up my own music management business which seems to be doing well. Mummy and I often pass each other in the hall, me going out to work, she coming home. A few months ago, when we were both at work, our flat was burgled and many items of great sentimental value were stolen, including jewellery given to me by a close friend who died and my mother's much-loved silver teapot. We were upset at the time, but within days we were over it. There are worse things in life than losing a silver teapot.

I returned to England via Zambia on 18 July. A personal appeal by Zambian President Kenneth Kaunda to Saddam Hussein on my behalf seemed to have paid dividends. Political analysts have since speculated that other pressures were brought to bear on the Iraqi leader, and that appearing to respond to Kaunda's request for clemency let him off the hook. Michelle had continued to campaign for my release relentlessly, appearing regularly on television and in magazines, and this way he could get rid of me without losing face. That theory would certainly fit with all we now know of him. Others have aired their opinion that Tiny Rowlands, the millionaire owner of the *Observer*, which employed Farzad on a freelance basis, used his influence to secure my release, or that the British Government put in a special request. I really don't know, and I have been stonewalled at every attempt to get to the bottom of the riddle. I now accept that I will probably never know the truth.

I spent my first night of freedom in a luxurious suite of rooms at the Zambian State House in Lusaka. I was told that the Queen had occupied the suite and slept in the enormous double bed during a state visit to Zambia, but unfortunately, by now accustomed to my hard prison bed, I found the royal bed much too soft for comfort and before morning I was forced to pull my blankets on to the floor. One luxury that was not wasted on me was the opulent bathroom. I filled the huge bathtub to the brim with hot water, added perfumed bubble bath and reclined for hours, letting the grime of the months seep from my pores. When the bath cooled I climbed out and refilled it again and again, until at last I felt clean.

My arrival in London remains a whirl. We touched down at Gatwick airport at around 5 a.m: all I can remember is Martina running up the steps of the aircraft and falling into my arms. Behind her came scores of reporters with cameras and microphones. Soon afterwards we were whisked away to an hotel in the Sussex countryside, courtesy of the *Observer*, where we were guests at a magnificent family party before spending two relaxing weeks with several former colleagues of Farzad who wanted to interview me for the paper.

I still recall those two weeks as being somehow strange and unreal. The weather was as beautiful as the countryside around us – lovely long, warm, summer days with nothing to do except enjoy ourselves. Michelle looked wonderful: I felt I could see the traces of strain disappear from her face as each day went by. She was obviously very much at home in the company of these media people, chattering animatedly, playing tennis, discussing issues I had forgotten existed. I was again reminded what a self-assured young woman she had become.

It was not easy to adapt to my new-found liberty. Sometimes I would sit and watch what was going on around me, in the hotel restaurant or the bar, and feel like an outsider. I knew my real place was here with these people, yet I still felt uneasy. Food was another problem. Much to everyone's amusement I chose to eat lamb every single day. In my months of imprisonment I had regularly dreamed of sitting down to a huge meal of lamb and mint sauce and now, with almost every imaginable dish on offer, it was all I wanted to eat. Although I enjoyed every morsel, I suspect that it represented another aspect of my attempt to convince myself of the truth that I was once again a free woman.

Of all the delights release had to offer, I think walking back into my London flat was the most thrilling of all. How many hours had I spent in my lonely cell visualising the bathroom with its old Victorian bath standing on four clawed feet, the kitchen with its old gas stove, the kettle in which I had made a thousand cups of tea, not to mention the view from my window? When I first stood in the middle of my sitting-room I wept with joy.

Just three weeks after my release the Iraqi Army marched into

Kuwait City. I spent the days and nights glued to the television and radio. I knew Saddam Hussein would not back down, but I didn't know whether the Allied troops would stick to their guns and oust him from the capital by force. I was mesmerised as I saw one familiar Baghdad building after another razed to the ground. When I watched the Allied bombing of the Fourteenth of July Bridge, over which I used to travel several times a week to visit the British Club or another expatriate haunt on my evenings off, I felt a part of me had disappeared with it beneath the surface of the River Tigris.

When I was imprisoned Baghdad had just been emerging from the devastation of its nine-year war with Iran. Things were beginning to come back into the shops and, after years of harsh rationing and supporting a rampant black market, the ordinary people were once again able to purchase foodstuffs and other commodities freely from local shops. The Gulf War brought an end to all that, and to see all the endeavours of the people of Iraq crushed by one man was horrendous for me. Leaders or governments make decisions, but it's the people in the street who lose their relatives and whose food and water supplies are cut off.

Since then I have made repeated efforts to find out about my friends in the prison, using both official and underground sources. No one has been able to help. The Red Cross continue to do what they can, but since the war it is difficult to get information about free men and women in Iraq, let alone 'convicted' criminals. Throughout the war and every day since I have wondered how or if they survived the conflict. The prison is south of Baghdad on the main route to Kuwait, the route the Allied bombers attempted to obliterate. The women relied on the water-cart coming into the prison every day and on the daily visit of the 'honey-wagon' to collect sewage, and I knew that once the road had been bombed both of these services would stop. The prison was always short of water and I could not imagine how they would survive. On the rare occasions when the 'honey-wagon' did not appear, sewage would flow out of the drains and into the courtyard and other communal areas.

Additionally, all the women depended on their relatives to supply them with food. Without the roads and most of the bridges connecting the city with the southern shore of the Tigris, how would their visitors get across? Images of the deprivation they must have suffered, and probably still are suffering, continue to haunt me. I wonder if Senna ever returned and, if she didn't, what punishment the hated Mohammed would be wreaking on the women now, especially Elizabeth, whom he so despised for being a Christian. Perhaps she has been 'persuaded' to convert to Islam – if, of course, she is still alive.

Since my release I have been actively involved with Prisoners Abroad, an organisation committed to the welfare of British Prisoners held in foreign prisons throughout the world; and with Fair Trials Abroad, which aims to draw up a series of international guidelines to ensure that any expatriate tried in a foreign court will obtain certain basic rights, including access to a lawyer within forty-eight hours, the presence of an independent observer who will report back to the defendant's country of origin, and various other considerations that most of us regard as a right rather than a privilege. I now know from personal experience how vital the work of these organisations is.

One high spot of the weeks following my release was an invitation from President Kenneth Kaunda to return to Zambia with Michelle and spend three weeks there as guests of the State. We jumped at his offer. Both of us felt in need of a holiday and it gave us the chance, without any outside pressures, to talk about what had happened and how we felt we would cope with the future. Then it was back to London and reality.

Almost immediately I began looking for work. I wrote to agencies and hospitals all over the world; I applied to clinics, rehabilitation centres and almost every hospital in the central London area to ask them if they had any vacancies. The answer was always the same: 'Sorry, nothing at the moment.'

I had given interviews to nursing magazines and journals and I feel this may have spoiled my chances: hospitals do not want the sort of publicity that employing 'celebrity' staff involves. They may also have feared that after my experience in Iraq, including almost a year out of uniform, I would not be up to the strenuous requirements demanded of nurses the world over.

The problem of unemployment loomed large in those early days, but eventually I was taken on as a freelance by a nursing agency and I am still on their books. One day I might be working in the intensive-care unit of a central London hospital, the next in a hospice or even on a building site. When there is no work available, I sit at home waiting for the telephone to ring, but something usually turns up.

For the future, I have no definite plan. I will continue with my nursing career, which pays the bills and allows me to keep my head above water, although I have enjoyed working on this book and would like to write another – perhaps a racy novel set among the expatriate community of a Middle East state. I continue to look for jobs abroad and, to the astonishment of many of my friends and family, I have made enquiries about finding employment in hospitals in the Gulf states. Despite my experiences I continue to feel a great fondness for the Middle East and its people. It was not they who were responsible for what happened to Farzad and myself; it is not they who are responsible for the atrocities that continue to be perpetrated in the prisons.

My attitude to life has changed enormously since my arrest and imprisonment in Iraq. If the months in jail have taught me anything, they have taught me that life is for the living and that every moment spent doing just that is truly precious. I no longer count the hours until the end of my shift or wish away the days until the weekend – I'm too busy getting the best I can out of every minute of today. And if tomorrow should bring the offer of a nursing job in Kuwait, Bahrain or Abu Dhabi, I'd take it like a shot. My suitcase is at the ready.

Acknowledgements

I have many, many people to acknowledge for their support during my imprisonment and since.

First and foremost – thanks to Peter Schwier and David Mukerji, who were such a source of comfort to Michelle and Martina throughout the ordeal, and to our family, including Brenda English, Erica and Fred Rogers, Mae and Alan Perry, Joyce and John Chivers, Cory de Vries, Edna Davies, Moira Hamilton and John Parish, all of whom suffered great anguish but whose love and loyalty never wavered. I will never be able to repay them.

In the UK, June Ball gave up family holidays to be on call twenty-four hours a day to give comfort and advice to Michelle and Martina. Thanks also go to Anne Wake and June Abbott, who set up a special fund-raising committee, to Dianne Hodges and Gillian Jones, who acted as legal adviser and press officer respectively, and to Jacqueline Baker, Joy Baker, Gillian Meadowcroft, Adrian Morris, John Ratings and Janet Robson. Friends who campaigned tirelessly on my behalf include Gwyneth and Edward, Sue Bath, Eileen Conley, Pam Cook, Greta Cooper, Sylvia Faulkner, Rene Fawley, Phyllis Heitman, Audrey Kennard, Margo Miller, Ralph Newberry, Trixie Newberry, Elisabeth Noll, Jo Parnal, Rose Pylnikow, Pauline Rogers, Sue Shaw, Sheena Verloe and Mary Watt.

For the work they did in Iraq, I should like to thank the British Ambassador and his wife, Harold (Hookey) Walker and Ann Walker; the First Secretary, Robin Kealy, who had to give me the news of Farzad's execution; and Consul Pauline Waugh, whom I first met as an official but soon came to regard as a friend. The counselling of the Venerable Michael Mansbridge, Archdeacon of the Gulf, allowed me, at last, the peace of mind for a nightmare-free sleep. Finally, my thanks to all my friends at the Ibn Al Bitar Hospital, including Director of Nursing Anne Morgan, Project Manager Paul Coleman, Audrey Lunn, Marion Noone, Helen O'Neill and Helena Tuite.

After my release the plane touched down briefly in Khartoum where I was met by John Beaven, the British Ambassador to the Sudan. My conversation with him brought home to me the realisation that I was free. Next stop was Zambia, where I had an audience with the President, Kenneth Kaunda, a kind, fatherly figure who had been instrumental in obtaining my release and whose personal assistant, Gloria Sleep, ensured my comfort during my first night of freedom in Lusaka. British Ambassador H.E. Peter Hinchliffe and his wife

Archie entertained me and made arrangements for me to meet members of the international press corps, some of whom had travelled over nineteen hours to speak to me.

It was only after my return to London that I fully realised the extent of the support received by Michelle. We cannot thank everyone but Michelle would especially like to mention officials at the Middle East Department of the Foreign and Commonwealth Office, Foreign Office Minister William Waldegrave, King Hussein of Jordan and some members of the British Press, particularly Adel Darwish and Harvey Morris of the *Independent* and Donald Trelford, Julie Flint, Peter Hillmore, Martin Huckerby, John McGhie and John Merritt of the *Observer*. Jon Scammell from TV AM was a particular source of good advice and friendship. As well as her father Cory de Vries, Michelle would like to single out her friends Stick, Greg, Richard V, Richard E, Julian, Frances, Jeremy, Alex, Kerris, Maria, Julia, Caroline, the rest of the Luckley girls and Arnold the cat. Special thanks go to John, whose friendship helped her adjust to life after our ordeal, and to Shirley Richter for her help and understanding. Michelle's love and gratitude also go to Pete.

Soon after my release I was contacted, via the *Observer*, by literary agent Faith Evans, who encouraged me to write up a draft of my experiences with a view to finding a suitable collaborator. Adel Darwish, the journalist who first broke the story of the explosion at Hilla, mentioned Pat Lancaster, Deputy Editor of *Middle East Magazine*. From our very first meeting Pat and I worked closely together, turning what might have been an extension of the nightmare into something that came nearer to therapy than anything that had been available to me since my release. Pat would like to acknowledge the patience and encouragement of her daughter Annabelle, as well as other members of her family including Rhona Wells and Barbara and Daniel Bannister. She would also like to thank Graham Benton and Alison Hutchins, her colleagues at *Middle East Magazine*, and Cherry and Rachel Perkins, who provided her with a quiet space to work in and much more.

Our collective thanks go to Faith Evans, whose exceptional talents as agent, editor and organiser kept the whole team together and brought the book to fruition. Her colleague Rosie Gilbey was a great source of support in her own right.

At Chapmans we would like to acknowledge the help and enthusiasm of Marjory and Ian and all their staff, especially Charlotte, Christine, David, Greg, Julia and Susan.

Finally I would like to extend my deepest gratitude to family, friends, colleagues, neighbours and the many hundreds of strangers from all over the world who wrote to me in Iraq and after my release with messages of support and love. My apologies, too, to the many people who, for reasons of their own safety, must remain anonymous – particularly to the women I left behind me in prison in Baghdad.

DAPHNE PARISH
May 1992